Backsli

Develop Your Staying Power

DAG HEWARD-MILLS

Parchment House

Unless otherwise stated, all Scripture quotations are taken from the King James Version of the Bible.

BACKSLIDING

Quotations from *Last Words of Saints and Sinners*.
Used by permission of Kregel Publications

First published by Parchment House 1998

Published by Lux Verbi.BM (Pty) Ltd. 2008

Published by Parchment House 2011
19th Printing 2018

[77]Find out more about Dag Heward-Mills
Healing Jesus Crusade
Write to: evangelist@daghewardmills.org
Website: www.daghewardmills.org
Facebook: Dag Heward-Mills
Twitter: @EvangelistDag

ISBN: 978-9988-7798-0-1

Dedication:
To my big sister, *Beatrix Ayache*
Thanks for your support through the years.

Contents

CHAPTER 1

What Is Backsliding?

God raised up the Prophet Jeremiah at a time when Israel and Judah were about to be taken captive in Babylon. He used Jeremiah to show the people of Israel the *backslidden state of their hearts.*

Jeremiah, Why Are You Crying?

The Book of Jeremiah gives several vivid descriptions of the backslidden state. Jeremiah, also known as "the weeping prophet", had most of his messages centered on the theme *backsliding*. He was often at "war" with the people of Israel, constantly warning them to repent and change from their wicked ways. The weeping prophet was concerned about the wayward attitude of his people. He repeatedly urged them, "Turn away from your wicked ways. Stop doing evil! Repent and come back to God."

He attempted to show them in many different ways what it meant to backslide. Yet the people of Israel and Judah refused to change.

Many years ago I learnt through experience that backsliding can be likened to walking on a road with no

signboards. In our Christian walk there are no signboards to warn you that you are backsliding. There is no sign that says, HELL AND DESTRUCTION - 200 METERS AHEAD. There's simply no such sign! **Backsliding happens gradually, until you are drawn somewhere you never expected to be. Gradually but certainly, you SLIDE there.**

Backsliding is real and can be analyzed by studying the different forms of backsliding described by Jeremiah. The prophet used real-life situations to describe this very common spiritual phenomenon. It is a common occurrence in the Christian world.

The Bible says,

> **...for many be called, but few chosen.**
> **Matthew 20:16**

In other words, many start out with Christ but many still fall away. The Bible also says,

> **...he that endureth TO THE END shall be saved.**
> **Matthew 10:22**

Many who come to Christ, fall away later.

Even YOU Can Backslide!

Some people may scorn at this topic and say, "I can't see myself backsliding." This very attitude shows that you are prone to backsliding. The Bible cautions in 1 Corinthians 10:12, **"Wherefore let him that thinketh he standeth take heed lest he FALL."**

This book will help you to develop staying power for the Christian race. **The more you know, the safer you will be - and the more staying power you will have.**

The Bible says,

> **...for we are not ignorant of his devices.**
> **2 Corinthians 2:11**

The teaching that this book offers will drive away the plague of ignorance. **Remember that those who do not read are no better than those who cannot read.** In other words, those who refuse to seek knowledge are no better than those who genuinely do not have the ability to do so.

In the next chapter, I am going to show you different ways by which you can look at backsliding.

CHAPTER 2

Bible Descriptions
of Backsliding

Exchanging Fountains for
BROKEN CISTERNS

…they have forsaken me the fountain of living waters, and hewed them out cisterns, broken cisterns, that can hold no water.

Jeremiah 2:13

When I was a medical student, I was sent on a working visit to Danfa, a Ghanaian village, for two weeks. Once, during a field trip, we came across another remote village that had no running water. Since the village had no running water, they had dug a large hole in the ground where water gathered; *often, this water was dirty and brownish.*

They Drank the Dirty Brown Water!

The people in the village bathed, defecated and urinated in it. At the same time they drank from it and used it to cook. This water obviously gave them various diseases and sicknesses.

In the Bible, backsliding people are likened to people who have access to clear running water, but exchange it for dirty smelly water - just like what I saw in that village.

I am sure you would wonder why someone would leave sweet, fresh, infection-free water, for sickness-infested and dirty water. There are believers who have had access to a life of holiness and godliness. However, they have rejected that to live a sinful and demon-controlled life.

God has given you an alternative to the dirty brown water. God is telling you that when you backslide you are going back to something terrible which will eventually kill you. He is telling you not to do something as absurd as drinking that muddy water again.

Becoming a Degenerate Wild Vine

...art thou turned into the degenerate plant of a strange vine...?

Jeremiah 2:21

The next Bible description of backsliding is that of a good plant which has degenerated into a thorny and strange vine.

Here, God shows us how a farmer's plantation from which he was expecting a good yield turned into a field of thorns and useless weeds.

You, the believer, are that beautiful plant of the Lord. Why on earth would you want to allow yourself to degenerate into a thorny and worthless shrub? This is how God sees you when you backslide.

God's problem with Israel was that He had invested so much love, care, tenderness and time into their lives. Yet they had turned into disobedient, hardhearted and wicked people. Will you allow yourself to become a worthless creature before God? The answer should be a definite "No!"

Becoming a Wild Camel

...thou art a swift dromedary traversing her ways.
Jeremiah 2:23

A backsliding Christian is also described as a *swift dromedary traversing her ways.* A dromedary is another name for a camel. It is a wild and swift creature, which strays anywhere.

The heart of a backsliding person is as unrestrained as a wild camel. It is not under the control of anything. It is loose and wild. I remember some years ago I went to visit a backsliding Christian in London.

My Friend Had Gone Wild

The best way I could describe this person was *loose and wild.* I was trying to bring him back to the Lord. It took me a long time to locate his house. I eventually got to his flat after midnight. He was surprised to see me, and welcomed me into his home. As we got to talking, he realized why I had come. Being a one-time mature Christian who had backslidden, he knew all the Scriptures I intended to quote.

So at a point he interrupted me and said, "Listen, I know what you are going to say, and I know all the Bible verses you are armed with tonight. But I want you to know that I don't really care."

So he took out his cigarette and started smoking right in front of me. He said, "I want you to see me smoking. Because I am not under any restrictions."

Then he took out an album and showed me some pictures he had taken with his girlfriend. Some of these pictures were quite suggestive and lewd.

He said, "I want you to see me as I really am. This is how I am now. This is what I do. And there is nothing anyone can do about it!"

Once again he was making the point that he could do anything he wanted to, and that no one could control him. **You see, backsliders are like wild camels which have no restrictions and boundaries anymore.** Your Christian life is supposed to be governed by God's Word.

When a person backslides he begins to do what he wants to do, and not what *God* wants him to do. He's like a wild animal with no checks and controls. God's Word gives us guidelines that are for our own good but a backslider chooses to live outside God's law. What a pity!

Becoming a Wild Ass

A wild ass used to the wilderness, that snuffeth up the wind at her pleasure; in her occasion who can turn her away...
Jeremiah 2:24

I prefer the Berkeley translation of this verse, which says:

Like a wild donkey accustomed to the wilderness, in the heat of her passion snuffing up the wind: in the time of her mating who can turn her lust away?
Jeremiah 2:24 (New Berkeley Version)

Many backsliders are like wild animals heated up with passion looking for a mate. The Amplified Bible puts it this way: **No**

males seeking her need weary themselves; in her month they will find her seeking them.

She Told Me, "I Have No Time For You!"

I remember one time going on a visit to search out a backsliding sister. I went with a good friend of mine, with whom I was doing some pastoral work . When we got to this backsliding sister's house, I told her that we had come to find out how she was doing in the Lord. Her house was in a part of the city I didn't know very well and it had taken us about three hours to find the house.

When we got there she looked at me with a straight face and said, "I cannot talk to you now because I am cooking."

Then I said, "We have come a long way to see you, and won't you even offer us a seat?"

She insisted that she had no time for us. So after mumbling a hurried exhortation to stay with the Lord, we scurried off. This young girl, who had no time for us, found time for an unbeliever boy who was 'chasing' her. She had no time for the Christian brothers who wanted to help her in her spiritual life. But the unbeliever boyfriend had no problem gaining access to her.

The Moffatt translation of the Bible elaborates further: **"No male need trouble to search for her; all can find her at mating time."**

When you become a backsliding Christian, the Bible says you become prey to unbelievers. Unbelievers can easily lead you away to sin.

Show me a backsliding Christian, and I'll show you an easy prey for the devil and his cohorts.

Satan capitalizes on the fleshly passions of backsliders, and has little problem finishing them off.

A Lady Who Forgets Her Ornaments

Can a maid FORGET her ORNAMENTS... yet my people have forgotten me...

Jeremiah 2:32

According to Jeremiah, the backslidden person is like a woman who forgets to put on her *ornaments.*

Many women are attached to their earrings, necklaces and make-up. Some women will never appear in public without adorning themselves with these accessories. (Unfortunately, many ladies substitute outer beauty for inner beauty. They have no time to pray, or read their Bibles but they spend a lot of time putting on all sorts of ornaments everyday!)

I must say I have rarely seen a lady who is not attached to her trinkets. **God compares the backslidden person to a young lady who has forgotten to beautify herself with her numerous dresses, shoes, necklaces, earrings, mascara and the rest. How unusual!**

Jeremiah realized that these things were part and parcel of every normal woman, and that women were very attached to these trappings.

He likened this bond between a woman and her ornamental accessories to the relationship that exists between a believer and God.

God describes the act of backsliding as a woman forgetting her ornaments.

In other words, backsliding and going away from God is a very unusual thing.

It may not look unusual in the natural, but in the sight of God and the angels it is a very strange phenomenon indeed.

Some people remind me of this very thing. Once upon a time they used to sing, praise, worship and even lead other Christians.

Today, They Are Just Nominal Christians

Today, they are just nominal Christians. One thing I am sure of, is that some Christians do not even know that they are backslidden.

If a vibrant charismatic Christian leader becomes just a nominal principled individual in society, he must understand that he has backslidden. Although people may consider him a good person, in the sight of God he is fallen from the high state that he used to be in - leading people to the Lord, exhorting them, sharing the Word, laying hands on people and so on.

One person comes to mind every time I think of this scripture. She was a vibrant, witnessing and fruitful Christian.

"Oh Pastor, We Still Go to Church"

Now and again, when I see her I ask, "How is your christian life?"

She smiles and says, "Oh Pastor, we still go to church."

All I can say for her is that she is a good and moral person who does no harm to anything or anyone. **But there used to be more to her Christianity than that!** Can a person who was so attached to the active, fruit-bearing Christian experience be separated from this state so easily? I wonder how the heavenly cloud of witnesses feel when they see this happen. Jeremiah could only describe it in one way - a woman separated from her ornaments.

A Bride Who Forgets Her WEDDING GOWN

Can a maid forget her ornaments, or a BRIDE her ATTIRE...

Jeremiah 2:32

Many brides are in love with their wedding gowns. Before the wedding day, they hang them in their wardrobes to ensure that they don't get stained.

Often, the gown is prepared in advance for the great day (and some gowns cost more than a year's salary!).

The bride's gown is worn for only a few hours, but the bride spares no expense when she is buying it. Many women are thrilled to be the bride - the star of the day, the most beautiful woman of the day, the princess of the moment. She walks down the aisle in splendor!

No Woman Forgets Her Wedding Gown!

God is saying that when you go away from Christ, you are like a bride who forgot to wear her wedding gown on her wedding day. I think if this were ever to happen it would enter the "Guinness Book of Records"! If anyone reading this has ever heard of a bride going for her wedding forgetting to put on her wedding gown, please write to me immediately!

This is why God is so horrified when Christians forget their God and backslide. It is simply implausible, inconceivable, and beyond belief. The Bible maintains that a bride cannot be divorced from her wedding dress. No! And that is why God was horrified when *you* first showed signs of backsliding.

A Lover Playing the Harlot

...thou hast PLAYED THE HARLOT with many lovers...

Jeremiah 3:1

God compares the backslider to a woman who is married to the man of her dreams, but then decides to go after other men. She jumps over the wall at night, leaves her dear, beloved, charming prince in bed and goes to hunt for "fresh blood".

I know that many people find the profession of prostitution horrifying and repulsive. They cannot imagine how people can abuse their bodies for a living.

I remember a lovely woman who had a respectable husband. After some years of marriage, this lady began to have affairs with

11

other men. She would climb over the wall and run away at night, when her noble husband was asleep. Can you imagine that?

But let me ask you something else. If your wife not only left you, but went out into the streets to become a prostitute, would that not even be worse? How would it feel like to pass by the 'red light' district and discover your wife busily trading her wares?

You would be shattered!

This is exactly how God feels when He sees the children He so loves standing out there in the world and selling themselves to the works of Satan. How sad!

Eating Your Own Vomit

As a dog returneth to his vomit, so a fool returneth to his folly.

Proverbs 26:11

When it comes to food I am very particular about what I eat. My mother always gave me piping hot food, so I am not used to eating food that is not very hot. I have decided not to eat anything I don't want to eat.

I remember once during a visit to the Far East, I sat at table with some dignitaries.

I must admit it was a very difficult experience for me having to swallow a few morsels of what looked like eels, snakes, clams and so on.

God knows how difficult it is for us to eat things we do not like. For most of us there are things we just wouldn't eat, even if we were starving. For example, your own vomit.

I recall one particular day when I saw a dog in my house vomiting some disgusting, pudding-like substance.

The Dog Ate the Strange Pudding

It was so smelly I just avoided that area of the house. **About an hour later, I passed by and I was very shocked to find the dog eagerly lapping up the pudding of vomit.** How utterly disgusting! I wondered why the dog was eating it. Was there no other food?

Some of you must have seen this phenomenon before. Well, that is *exactly* what you look like when you go back to your old ways, old boyfriends, old girlfriends and old habits you once vomited out. God is utterly surprised at you.

This reminds us of the prodigal son who ended up eating pig feed. The prodigal son is another description of the backslidden believer. He demanded his share of his father's property and walked out of his father's house. He journeyed to a far country and wasted all his substance on riotous living. In the end he had to feed with pigs.

And he would fain have filled his belly with the husks that the swine did eat...

Luke 15:16

And that is what it means to backslide. **If you have the opportunity to eat at table with your Christian family, why must you end up eating with pigs?**

Dear Christian friend, I have tried in these last few pages to describe the horrors of backsliding as graphically as I possibly can. What else can I say? If this message is not clear to you, you may either be deaf, blind or simply dishonest. God is telling us clearly that once we have come to know Him, we will do well to stay with Him. There is no turning back and no falling away.

But we are not of them who draw back unto perdition...
Hebrews 10:39

...No man, having put his hand to the plough, and looking back, is fit for the Kingdom of God.
Luke 9:62

CHAPTER 3

Principal Causes of Backsliding

I know that there are many causes of backsliding, but in this chapter, I will try to give you the predominant causes, as the Lord has shown me.

Shallowness

... and these have NO ROOT, which for a while believe...

Luke 8:13

The parable of the sower gives various reasons why some of the seeds could not grow. Some seeds could not grow because they fell on rocky soil.

Jesus explained that these are the ones who receive the Word of God with joy, and even believe for a while. But in the time of testing, they fall away because they have no root.

Everyone Will Be Tested

A time of testing will surely come for every Christian. If you are *shallow*, in the time of testing, you will fall. Through experience I have noticed that many Christians do not have

14

deep roots. They do not know God for themselves. They cannot even explain why they do the things they do. They don't know why they belong to a particular church. They do not know why they speak in tongues. They do not even know why they give offerings. When they face a little criticism, they get confused and have no defense.

Having no personal experience with God, these are the people who can never say, "God spoke to me." **They have no convictions of their own.**

A close friend who brought me up in the Lord deviated from Christianity, and became a member of a cult. But I did not follow him into that cult because I had my own deep-rooted convictions.

I know why I am serving the Lord, and so my father, mother or closest friend cannot change my mind. **Many Christians who are not rooted in sound biblical doctrine can easily be persuaded to follow fables**. Some born-again believers fall away because they do not know the difference between the true gospel, and the beliefs of sects like the Jehovah Witnesses.

I Witnessed to the Jehovah's Witness

Once, I was standing at the Thomas Sankara Circle in the city of Accra when a Jehovah's Witness came up to me to try to convert me to his faith.

He asked, "Do you believe in the Holy Spirit?"

I replied, "I certainly do!"

Then I asked him, "Have *you* heard of 'speaking in tongues'?"

He said, "Yes. But I don't believe in it."

So I asked him, "What is *this*...?"

Then I released a string of tongues in the direction of this sincere (but sincerely wrong) gentleman.

This ended our conversation. He fled! If I were not convinced that speaking in tongues is an ability which comes with the Holy

Spirit, he could have confused me. But I knew my Bible, and I knew (as I still do today) that the Holy Spirit is from God, and speaking in tongues is one of his gifts.

Don't just speak in tongues because others are speaking in tongues. You must know why tongues sounds like a monotonous and repetitive language. It is because the Bible says, "with a stammering tongue will I speak to you". Tongues is described as a stammering tongue. It is not just an ordinary language. It is a heavenly language that comes out in a stammering fashion.

Will You Fall at the Next Crisis?

You may be in a church, but if you are not "deep" you will fall away at the next shaking and crisis. Next time there is a problem in the church, your membership and commitment will be shaken. Only a *"shallow"* Christian would fall away when a great man of God gets into some scandalous sin. **What have the sins of that man of God got to do with your own salvation? Why on earth would you think of leaving Christ because of your pastor's mistakes?** Christians behave in this way because they themselves are shallow!

Don't Follow Me, If I Don't Follow Christ

I am the pastor of a very large church. I know many people would do anything I tell them to. But I always tell my church members not to follow me if I do not follow Christ. After all, I am also a man, and can make mistakes. I tell them, "If I tell you to do something that is not biblical, do not do it. Only do things which can be supported by the Bible."

If you are not sure about anything your pastor is saying, just ask him, "Please Sir, what is the scriptural basis for this new revelation?"

Not abiding by this principle is the reason why some so-called pastors can bathe their members in the nude (what they call 'holy' baths). Some so-called ministers are also able to dupe people out of all their earthly possessions.

This is because the pastors know that they are dealing with shallow people.

Paul said, "Follow me as long as I follow Christ". He was a man subject to like passions, so whatever he did had to be scrutinized by the book of books: The Bible!

Did you know that Aaron led the people of Israel to build a golden calf after God had delivered them from Egypt? These people were saved all right, but were shallow in their experience with God. When Moses was held up on the mountain, the Israelites in their shallow faith, turned shortly to idols and declared, "These be thy gods, O Israel, which brought thee up out of the land of Egypt."

Don't be shallow and light, blown about by every wind of doctrine! Don't just follow the crowd! It is shallow people who just follow the crowd.

Following the Crowd Can Be Dangerous

Many became calf worshippers in the days of Aaron because they followed the crowd.

Many murmured and were destroyed in the days of Moses and the ten spies because they followed the crowd.

Many got involved in the killing of Jesus, the Son of God because they followed the crowd.

Following the crowd can be dangerous!

Don't be a shallow Christian. Be deep. Don't be a believer for just a while.

Let your roots grow deep. As the songwriter says, *"Draw me deeper, Lord!"*

Emptiness

... I am no better than ECHOING bronze...
1 Corinthians 13:1 (Ronald Knox Translation)

The word *echo* in this Scripture comes from the emptiness I am talking about in this section of the book. There are many Christians who are empty. There is nothing in them. I call them *"airy Christians"*. They have little or no Word in them, neither are they full of the Holy Spirit or of love. They may speak in tongues, but the Bible says whenever they do so, they are just making a lot of noise

I think the Ronald Knox Translation of 1 Corinthians 13:1, which I have quoted above, really brings out the concept of *spiritual emptiness*. If I have no love "I am no better than echoing bronze or the *clash* of cymbals." I say once again, the *echo* and the *clash* are a result of the emptiness within.

Empty Christians Are Targets

Emptiness will attract other things to fill that empty space. A spiritual vacuum will be filled with spiritual things, either positively or negatively. Nature abhors a vacuum, and every space will be filled.

And when he [an evil spirit] cometh, he findeth it UNOCCUPIED...
Luke 11:25 (Goodspeed Translation)

Empty Christians are targets for the enemy. The devil will try to fill you with evil and backsliding tendencies because of the emptiness within you.

... and they chose Stephen, a man FULL of faith and of the Holy Ghost ...
Acts 6:5

As you can see, Stephen was full of something positive. That is why he did not backslide, but went on to become a great evangelist.

There is the saying that empty barrels make the most noise. These are the *echoes* 1 Corinthians 13 is talking about. This same principle definitely applies in Christianity. **Empty Christians are loud and noticeable but not substantial.** There is the need for every Christian to be filled with the Spirit, with love and with the Word.

What are you filling your spirit with? Fill your spirit with the Word of God, with faith, with good Christian music. (By the way don't mess around with non-christian music- it will fill your mind with junk!) **Fill your time with church activities. If you don't fill your life with these good things *something else* will fill it. Drive away the emptiness from your spiritual life.** This is a fundamental key to staying power for the Christian race.

Lust

For Demas hath forsaken me, having LOVED this present world...

2 Timothy 4:10

Demas loved the world. That is why he deserted Paul. If you love somebody, you will eventually gravitate towards that person. This explains why young ladies will leave their loving parents and marry virtual strangers. Love or lust is one of the reasons for that gravitational pull.

If you love the world- its money, its women, its men, its glitter - you will find yourself gravitating towards these things. It is therefore important that the Christian should not have any strange love in his heart.

I have one "love" for my Lord, and a second "love" for my wife. I cannot allow any other "love" to exist in my heart.

Strong Desires Are Dangerous!

There are many Christian ladies who have such strong desires to marry that they will sacrifice all principles and all the rules in order to get married. To lust after something is to have a strong, excessive desire for something.

Usually it is an uncontrollable, sometimes obsessive desire for a particular thing. One dictionary calls 'lust' an animal desire. Be wary of all forms of lust, whether it's financial lust, sexual lust or power lust. **Lust corrupts.** Remember the Scripture,

> ... having escaped the CORRUPTION that is in the world THROUGH LUST.
>
> **2 Peter 1:4**

The prodigal son had a strong desire for the world. He wanted to leave home so he could have the pleasures of the world. He was deceived and wanted something else. But there was nothing else! He soon found out that the situation out there was not as good as it was at home.

Often Christians feel they are missing out on something in the world. Sometimes they feel they are losing out on money, sex, glamour and so on. Apart from the love of Christ, if you have any other love in you, you need to be careful of it. **If you have any strange lusts in you, you must kill them now, or they will grow up and take over your life.**

I Killed it!

I once saw a baby snake in my garden. It looked very much like an ordinary worm but it was definitely a snake. So I said to myself, "If I don't kill it now, one day it could kill me." I thought, "It is too dangerous to leave this thing alive. Let me kill it now," I decided.

That is how we must deal with some of those desires lurking within us. Deal with them like I dealt with that snake. Kill them now, when they are small and harmless. If you allow them to grow and to develop, they will destroy you one day.

Bitterness

> ... lest any root of BITTERNESS springing up TROUBLE you ...
>
> **Hebrews 12:15**

20

Many people who walk out of a church are offended Christians who became bitter. They were probably genuinely offended, but their wounds never healed.

When my wife was pregnant with our second son, Joshua, I sometimes went with her to the antenatal clinic. To while away the time I engaged in conversation with one of the doctors. One morning as I chatted with this doctor, I noticed that one of his toes was missing.

He Had a Missing Toe

So I asked, "What happened to your toe?"

He answered, "I am a diabetic patient, and I once had an injury to that toe. (You know, the wounds of some diabetic patients don't easily heal)."

He continued, "I hit my toe on an object, but after some time the wound did not heal. This wound deteriorated until it affected my whole leg."

He lamented about how the doctors had even considered amputating his whole leg. However, in the end they decided to cut off only the toe in question."It was a very traumatic experience for me. That's how I ended up without a toe," he concluded.

As I mused over the story of this missing toe, the Spirit of God spoke to me and said, "This is what happens to Christians who get hurt and never fully recover from their hurts."

The Holy Spirit showed me how many Christians and pastors allow their hurts to degenerate into unhealed, gangrenous wounds of the heart. He continued, **"They separate themselves from other Christians in the name of being cautious and not wanting to be hurt all over again.**

This separation eventually leads to total isolation from the body of Christ - and backsliding."

Sometimes I think of all the hurts I've experienced in this ministry, and how they have tended to isolate me. I can remember when my former pastor offended me, and refused to support me when I started out in ministry!

None of Them Came to My Wedding

I invited all the pastors I knew to my wedding. But none of them attended. When it was time to take group pictures, the Master of Ceremonies called out for all pastors to come forward. But there was no one. I was totally rejected by the other ministers in the city.

A close family friend and neighbor once called me the leader of a cult! I have had trusted pastors betray me and turn against me. I have experienced mid-stream desertion in ministry by trusted people. I have had faithful church members I invested a lot in, fight against me!

I even decided at a point to stay away from interactions with many people. But, as I thought about this man's toe, I realized what was gradually happening to me. I was being cut off from the rest of the church in Ghana, just like this man's toe. And it was all because of unhealed wounds and hurts. I decided then to allow the wounds in me to heal.

I have noticed that there are many seniors in the ministry who have become disappointed, disillusioned, and unforgiving. I have watched as great ministers who once affected the whole nation, become isolated and cut off themselves from the rest of the body of Christ.

He Could Not Hide His Wounds From Me

One time I was in the office counselling, when a young man came to me.

He boldly stated, "I have decided to be in your church because I believe this is where God wants me to be."

I queried, "Why did you leave your former church?"

He replied, "I was led by the Spirit to come here."

I asked, "Apart from the Spirit's leading did anything else happen to make you decide to leave that church?"

He hesitated, "Well… there was a slight problem…" And he went on and on about problems that had arisen in his previous church.

I immediately knew that what I suspected was true. This man was hurt, and his unresolved hurts had caused him to be cut off from his church. **This is one of the commonest reasons for people backsliding and leaving churches.**

Backsliding Love!

Married couples also backslide in their relationships towards each other. They start out with hot, strong and fiery love, which is often blind and unseeing. **However, many couples after several years of marriage either just co-exist or even hate each other.**

How did they backslide from love to hatred? Often the hurts and offences of marriage were never fully resolved until they were virtually cut off from each other. This is one of the favorite tricks of the devil.

If he can isolate you through hurts, he will have the opportunity to speak to you and make you backslide. You see, you are more vulnerable when you are isolated. The book of Hebrews warns us that bitterness can trouble us greatly.

… lest any root of BITTERNESS springing up TROUBLE you…

Hebrews 12:15

Sinfulness

My son, if sinners entice thee, consent thou not.
Proverbs 1:10

Many of the Christians who walk out of church and backslide have often been living in sin.

Although they were in church, some of them used to commit fornication, adultery, stealing, and other sins. These are the church members who easily become annoyed with their pastors for preaching about their evil deeds. They do not want certain portions of the scriptures to be referred to. They feel uncomfortable when certain subjects are preached in church.

They Don't Like Hot Sermons

They also hate hard-hitting, Holy Ghost inspired messages that lay bare the realities of righteous living.

One morning, a friend of mine was chatting with her colleague in the office.

She asked him, "How was your week-end?"

"Oh, it was fine! I went to church on Sunday," he replied.

"How was church?" she asked.

He answered, "I'm not impressed with my church anymore. I don't think I'll go back there again."

She was surprised and wondered, "What's wrong with your church? You've been going there for sometime now."

He answered, "The pastor's sermons are not uplifting. I tell you, we are not blessed!"

He went on, "If he wants to preach, he should just preach. But all this going on about fornication, and people having girlfriends isn't necessary."

You see, this married man was having an affair with a young lady in the office and he didn't like his sin being exposed. I tell you, there was nothing wrong with that pastor's preaching. Fornication is a subject in the Bible which must be addressed.

Such Christians can easily leave church to avoid the confrontations of God's Word, instead of admitting their sins and repenting.

When a believer sins and acknowledges his mistake, he is on his way to being healed.

Address the sin in your life. Correct the mistakes. Deal with every evil thought and habit. This will keep you in the Lord. Sin is definitely a primary cause of backsliding.

My son, if sinners entice thee, consent thou not.
Proverbs 1:10

Without Truth

My parents taught me never to tell lies. My mother kept telling me throughout my childhood that my father didn't tell lies, so I was not supposed to tell lies. As I grew up I found it difficult to tell lies.

These six things doth the Lord hate...a proud look, A LYING TONGUE, and hands that shed innocent blood.
Proverbs 6:16,17

Liars are compared to wicked people who shed innocent blood. There are born again Christians who habitually lie through their teeth. They lie to God and to man without batting an eyelid.

Stand your ground then, with TRUTH for your belt...
Ephesians 6:14 (Twentieth Century New Testament)
This belt of truth holds the whole armour together. **Truth, honesty and sincerity are things that hold your entire Christian life together. Without sincerity your Christian life will disintegrate, and you will backslide.**

I remember being in a service once with some other brethren. There was a young lady who had been prophesying and holding up the whole service for periods of time.

The Demon-Possessed Girl

She would stand up whilst the leader was preaching, and interrupt the service with very long prophecies. She would command the priest to stop the administration of communion.

25

This young girl would prophesy and make the entire congregation kneel down and stand up at will.

Many of the leaders were inexperienced, and didn't know what to do. So they would stand back as this young lady dominated the entire service. I had been told about this young lady who had been controlling the meetings, but had never seen her myself.

That day, I realized that I was seeing the manifestation of an evil spirit "live". This young lady stood up and began to take over the service with her prophecies just as had been described to me. So I got out of my seat, took a couple of brothers with me, and escorted her into the basement of the building. I knew that an evil spirit was controlling this young lady. As soon as we got into the basement, this young lady's eyes widened and blazed.

She looked straight at me and said, "Do not quench the Spirit!"

I could virtually see the demons dancing in her eyes. This almost unsettled me as I wondered, *"Was I quenching the Spirit"*. Then I said, "You foul spirit, in the name of Jesus. I command you to stop your activities and come out of this girl."

She immediately went into all sorts of writhing movements. The spirit began to manifest, spoke to us using the girl's voice and said many things. I cannot give all the details of this deliverance episode in this book. However, there was one thing that struck me, which I want to highlight here.

I asked the demon spirit, "How did you come into this lady?"

That spirit said, *"The belt of truth was loose."*

The demons had gained access to this young girl's life because the protective armour of truth, sincerity and honesty was deficient in one way or the other.

I cannot tell you how exactly this girl's belt of truth was loosed. That is not important to you. What is important is your belt of truth.

Lying Opens the Gate to Evil Spirits

Are you honest? Are you sincere? When you make a mistake do you admit it easily? Are you truthful to yourself and to God? I tell you, there are many people who lie to themselves continually and tell themselves, "I am okay", when they know they are not.

Do not deceive yourself! Be honest and sincere! Be straightforward! Jesus said, "You will know the truth and the truth will make you free." Don't be angry when you hear the truth. It is the truth that you need.

Rebellion

There is one sin which is compared to witchcraft in the Bible. That is the sin of rebellion.

For REBELLION is as [like] the sin of WITCHCRAFT...
1 Samuel 15:23

Rebellion is the fight against all authority. Rebellion often camouflages itself as the fight for independence. Many so-called freedom and independence fighters are actually downright rebels.

Africa, for instance, has had its fair share of rebels. There have been rebellions and uprisings against governments all over Africa.

There are also many rebellious elements in the church. There are rebellious pastors who break out of their rightful positions as branch pastors, assistant pastors and so on.

There are rebellious church members who break out of their God-given places within churches. (I assure you that rebels usually have very spiritual reasons for the things they do!)

Rebellion stems from the heart. And every rebellious child of God has rejected legitimate authority in his life. The result therefore is backsliding. I have known Christians who do not want anything, be it human or divine, to instruct them concerning their lives. Rebellion is a cardinal factor in the backsliding phenomenon.

It was rebellion against his father's authority that led the prodigal son to leave home. The rebellion in the prodigal son's heart led him to eat with pigs. I am sure you don't want to end up eating with pigs. Don't be a rebel. All rebels are destined to end in one way. **Ask the prodigal son, ask Judas, ask Absalom, ask Adonijah, ask Ahithophel, ask Shimei, and ask Lucifer to tell you what happened to them when they rebelled.**

All rebels are headed for one judgement- EXECUTION!!

Foolishness

He that trusteth in his own heart is a FOOL...
Proverbs 28:26

Many Christians do foolish things. They venture into places only fools would dare. There are some situations, and some people who will lead you into trouble. Some young unmarried Christian couples court disaster when they engage in certain things.

Sometimes during courtship, some Christians can be found in 'unhealthy' situations after midnight. Then when you become pregnant before your wedding, you get surprised that you fell into sin! Why should you be surprised?

What Is a Business Lunch?

There are some ladies whose specialty is to wine and dine with married men. And their excuse is that they work with these men. "Oh, It's just a business lunch," they say.

But I tell you, they are playing with fire.

I have seen Christian brothers and sisters live in the same flat, and even in the same room, all in the name of saving money. The next thing that happened was they fell in 'love'. Then before you could say, "Jack Robinson" they had a baby. Foolishness has a price.

All things are lawful for me, but all things are not expedient...

1 Corinthians 10:23

Some types of behaviour are straightforward foolishness. **You should never overestimate your spiritual strength.**

God has continually drummed it into me that being a pastor does not make me immune or special. The Lord has made it clear that he will treat me as he treats everyone else.

So no matter who you are, if you walk in foolishness and absurdity you will backslide. It is as simple as that!

Fools make a mock at sin...

Proverbs 14:9

CHAPTER 4

The Psychology of Backsliding

The psychology of backsliding deals with the way backsliders think. It deals with the attitudes of a defecting Christian. You see, the Bible says we should guard our hearts with all diligence, for out of it are the issues of life.

Keep thy heart with all diligence; for out of it are the issues of life.

Proverbs 4:23

Backsliding is one of the issues of life. The issue of backsliding comes from the heart. A thought in the heart becomes an attitude. An attitude becomes an action. And these actions become behaviour patterns.

Let us look at the attitudes that form in the heart of a backslider. It is these attitudes that give him the false confidence in his backslidden state.

ATTITUDE #1

"I'm Not Alone, Others Are Backsliding Too."

I have noticed that one of the things we do, is to find out who else is in a condition similar to ours. And when we get involved in something we also try to take others with us (like drowning men). But the Bible says,

...every man shall bear his OWN burden.
Galatians 6:5

You may take confidence in the fact that others seem to be doing as badly as you are. But that is a false assurance.

I remember when I travelled to a city in Ghana and visited a brother whom I had known to be very zealous for the Lord. Unfortunately, this brother whom I even considered to be in the rank of a minister had backslidden, and had made a young lady pregnant. He no longer went to church regularly.

When my wife and I got to his house, we chatted a bit, and asked, "How are you doing spiritually?"

He said, "Oh, God is good."

Then he immediately changed the topic and asked whether we had heard about another good friend of ours who had backslidden terribly.

But My Condition Is Better Than His

"Brother X's condition is very unfortunate," he lamented.

He added, "Have you heard? He's fallen into very bad company, and doesn't go to church at all."

He was trying to make us see that this brother's condition was even worse than his.

As we were going home in the car, I asked my wife if she noticed that this brother seemed to have taken some reassurance in the fact that our other friend was in an even worse state.

You can tell when people are trying to reassure themselves. Just listen to the things they say. They say things like: *"Nowadays a lot of people don't go to church... City life is too busy for regular church attendance... There are now many Christians who drink a little beer with their food..."*

Dear friend, don't be deceived by the existence of a crowd. You may think that everybody is sinning just like you are. **But when Christ comes you'll be very surprised to find people whom you thought would go to hell with you, passing you by on their way to Heaven!**

A friend once told me about an incident that jolted him into becoming a Christian.

What?! Are You Also a Christian?

He told me, "I was a party-going, night-life person with lots of girlfriends. One day, I was going home in a friend's car after one of our usual parties when I noticed that the car was unusually quiet."

"So I decided to slot in some good old disco music to liven up the atmosphere. I picked up one of the tapes lying in the front of the car and inserted it. To my utmost surprise, instead of music, I heard the sound of preaching."

I exclaimed, "Hey, what's this? Since when did you start listening to such things? Are you also one of those born again people?"

And his friend replied, "Hey, I am securing myself."

My friend said to me "I began to think very fast; If our car was to have had an accident and we were both to die, he may have gone to *Heaven*, and I would have gone to *Hell*!!"

My friend suddenly realized that he had been deceived into thinking that everyone of his friends was a ruthless sinner like he was. People were secretly seeking God and securing their places in Heaven.

You better make sure that you are doing the right thing. Do not look at the crowd. You are born alone, and you will die alone. Do not even look to your husband or your wife. It is unusual for husbands and wives to be born on the same day. It is even more unusual for them to die on the same day.

You will stand before God as an individual. Never forget that fact of life.

ATTITUDE #2

"I Have a Lot of Time, Christ is Not Really Coming Soon."

The world is truly amused when we say that Christ is coming soon. They think it is a theory cooked up by some deranged people.

On the other hand, some Christians know that Christ's Second Coming is a reality. But they think that it won't happen very soon. At least, not in their lifetime. They suppose they can enjoy themselves and forget about the future. But what they forget is that Christ's coming will be a very *unexpected* event.

...The day of the Lord so cometh AS A THIEF IN THE NIGHT. For when they shall say, Peace and safety; then sudden destruction cometh upon them, as travail upon a woman with child; and they shall not escape.
1 Thessalonians 5:2-3

A pregnant woman who is due might be all right one moment,and the next moment, go into labour. Severe pain will strike her and a baby will be born. So will the coming of the Lord be. Everything will be all right one day and the next, total chaos in the world.

Jesus Could Come This Friday!

Jesus compares his coming to the coming of a thief. No one expects a thief. I remember years ago when thieves broke into my father's house. We were not expecting anything of the sort, but it just happened. The whole world will be very surprised when Jesus comes again.

Many of you have taken God's grace period of repentance for granted. Indeed, this grace period means nothing to some of us. **The grace period has rather become more time to play the "fool". This is how backsliders think.** *I have more time! I have much more time!!*

You may be planning to have your grand wedding. But it may never come on. Perhaps, those who are in school may never complete their courses. The trumpet will suddenly sound, and those of us who are washed in the blood of the Lamb, and ready for the Saviour would be caught up in the clouds to be with Him forever.

ATTITUDE #3

"There Are Short Cuts to Everything, Including Going to Heaven."

The world is under the delusion that there are short cuts to everything. Unfortunately, some Christians think in the same way. They assume that there must be some short cut to Heaven since there seems to be a short cut to almost everything.

I Learnt the Hard Way!

You cannot escape the Christian rudiments and go to Heaven. You cannot escape the cross. Jesus said, "Take up thy cross and follow me." There is no short cut around the cross. You must take it up. In this day and age of instant coffee, instant tea and jet travel, everybody wants to have things fast, quick and short.

When I was in boarding school, I learnt the hard way that short cuts must be avoided.

Those of us in the junior forms were asked to do some general scrubbing in school. I obtained an excuse duty slip from the doctor. It exempted me from any assigned duties for the next four days.

I happened to discuss this excuse duty slip with a friend, and excitedly told him how I wouldn't have to do any hard work for the next four days. Then he came up with what I thought was a bright idea.

He suggested, "Why don't you write "1" before the "4" so it reads "14" days instead of "4"? You will then have fourteen whole days to relax."

As I mused over this suggestion, I thought, "What a good idea! No one will notice."

The Day I Met My First Judas

But this friend was the first Judas I was to meet in my life.

After I had taken his suggestion and changed the '4' to '14', this same friend reported me to the seniors. He told them that I had forged my excuse duty slip.

Every one pounced on me, and I was charged. I tell you, I suffered greatly for that mistake. First of all, my four days of excuse were cancelled. I was given the most difficult jobs to do. And then I was given extra punishment.

From that time I decided: *No more short cuts in life.* I realized long ago that there was no short cut to Heaven. I will have to go the hard way.

We may think that there is a shorter way to Heaven, but there is only one way to Heaven. It is not through Allah, Islam, fetish, chanting or meditation. It is only by accepting the Lord Jesus Christ as your personal Saviour and being born again. There is no short cut.

In the secular world, wise businessmen are wary of any "get-rich-quick" schemes. Many however, are not tired of trying one quick scheme after the other. So they take advantage of every opportunity to make some quick money.

They Said, "Your Church Will Be Rich."

Someone once asked our church to join a new 'get-rich-quick' bank.

He explained, "As a growing church you will need a lot of money to help complete your building project."

But I immediately said, "It sounds too good to be true, and too quick to be real."

So we didn't join it.

A few weeks later, I heard of how that new bank had collapsed. Many people lost their money. I also heard of how some churches had lost huge sums of money by saving there.

The Bible says the Kingdom of Heaven is like a mustard seed, which needs time to grow to become a great tree. When you put the seed into the ground, it will need to go through the long process of dying and growing before yielding fruit. Unfortunately, some of us want to escape the processes of dying and growing up. **You cannot expect to just put money in the offering and hope that everything will be all right. You cannot avoid the reality of fasting, praying, fellowshipping and witnessing. These are Biblical standards we just cannot avoid!!**

ATTITUDE #4

"God Loves Me Too Much To Punish Me."

I have heard Christians say that God will never punish them. They quote, "For God so loved the world…"

They argue that since God loves the world so much He will not destroy them. They say, "I know God will forgive me." Because of this they add sin to sin without batting an eyelid.

Two Sides of a Coin

God's nature is like two sides of a coin. One side of the coin shows the head, and the other side shows the tail. **One side of God's character shows His great love, and the other side shows His judgement.**

A Christian sister spoke of a woman who was having an affair with her best friend's husband. Because the two ladies were good friends they would often speak on the phone. Every time this adulteress put the phone down, she would sigh and say, "O God, forgive me for what I'm doing."

Strangely, she still didn't stop destroying her friend's marriage. Some people feel that God will not punish them. That is why they continue in sin.

When God shows you one side of His character you will see love, forgiveness and mercy of the highest order. God will forgive and forget your sins. **But a time will come when God will show you the other side of His nature;** which is judgment, justice, fairness, equity and jurisprudence. These are the two sides of God's nature. We are now in the Dispensation of Grace. God is showing you mercy and love.

Think about all the wicked sins you have committed, but still receive His forgiveness. At a certain point, the Spirit of the Lord will not strive with man anymore. God has to judge you, otherwise there will be chaos in the Kingdom.

The king by judgment establisheth the land...
Proverbs 29:4

God loves you so much that He will punish you when He has to.

ATTITUDE #5

"I Have More Time, I'm Not Going To Die Soon."

People think that because they are young they still have a lot of time. Also they think they have enough of their lives ahead of them to sort things out with God.

I wrote this book at a time when the whole world shook at the news of the death of Princess Diana and her millionaire companion. No one in his wildest imagination would have thought that someone so young, so charming and so beautiful could be taken off the face of the earth so suddenly.

The security of an armour-plated Mercedes Benz with airbags all around could not prevent her death in a car accident in Paris. I tell you, none of us was expecting this!

Everyone thinks that there is more time. I'm sure Princess Diana thought there were many more years ahead. We all did. But it was not so. That is why the whole world trembled with shock. **It is not safe to assume that there is more time.** The Bible warns us that because we don't know the day or the hour Christ will come, we must *be ready* all the time. The key word here is preparation and readiness.

> **...thus will I do unto thee...because I will do this unto thee...PREPARE to meet thy God...**
>
> **Amos 4:12**

In Luke 12, the Bible tells the story of a man who had a successful business. He had so much that he wondered what to do with the profits. He decided to build bigger barns to store his goods. In our time this would be equivalent to opening new bank accounts. When he completed his projects, he said to himself, "Soul, thou hast much goods laid up for many years. Take thine ease, eat, drink and be merry."

Come Up for a Meeting

God reacted immediately from Heaven and said, "...This night thy soul shall be required of thee." In other words, I want to have a discussion with you tonight. **God has the right to call you up for a discussion at any time.** God is showing us here that there is just a step between us and death.

There are three times in your life when people will gather to honour you. They gather when you are born and christened. Then they gather again when you are getting married.

And finally, they will definitely also gather for you when you die. Somebody might contend that he or she is too young to die. But go to the mortuary, and you will discover that even little babies die. I was once in a hospital ward with one of my assistant pastors when we happened to see the body of a little baby who had just died. Although it was a tiny baby who had just began to live, it died. **That baby was not too young to die.**

Dear Christian friend, do not put off your godly obligations because you think you are still young and there is more time. **You never know when God will summon you to account for your life.**

...thus will I do unto thee,...because I will do this unto thee...PREPARE to meet thy God.

Amos 4:12

CHAPTER 5

Symptoms of Backsliding

And there shall be SIGNS...when ye see these things...
KNOW...

Luke 21:25-31

I n the field of medicine a symptom or sign is the outward clue of something dangerous. Often when you are searching for something that is hidden, you look out for clues to lead you. Symptoms and signs help doctors to make the right diagnosis.

Symptoms Reveal the Condition

A symptom is meaningless to the unlearned, but important to the learned. If a symptom is detected early it can save a life. When a doctor detects certain signs, he knows that the patient's life is in danger. But a layman may have no idea of what is going on.

When the hand of a patient shows certain signs, it is an indication of a serious disease in the liver. **What has the hand got to do with the liver? They are so far apart anyway.** But it may surprise you to know that a shaking and jerking hand could indicate liver failure. To the unlearned, that shaking hand is just an unusual spasm. Some may even think that it is a sign of the anointing!

The pancreas is located somewhere deep in the abdomen. How can you know whether the pancreas is working or not? The only way to know is to look out for certain symptoms or signs.

I once noticed a middle-aged person drinking a lot of water and passing a lot of urine. This person was fat and overweight. As a medical doctor I immediately thought, "Perhaps this person is diabetic and doesn't even know it. There may be something wrong with his pancreas." It was an important sign to me.

When you are learned in certain fields you will notice things that others do not.

As you read this book you will learn about some of the symptoms which give an indication that a person is backsliding spiritually. And this person may be you! May you become spiritually alert, and not take certain things for granted anymore after reading this section.

Symptoms of the Soul

As scientists search for signs to know what is going on inside the BODY of a man, we must also look for the signs that uncover what is happening inside the SOUL of a man.

The early detection of some of these symptoms can save a believer from backsliding and going to hell. Knowledge of the existence of these symptoms can give you staying power for the Christian race.

There is no point in regularly attending church, knowing the Lord, and later dying as a backslider! Why should I spend all my years preaching and later become a castaway? Why do the Lord's work today, and serve the devil tomorrow?

This is a picture of what happened to the five foolish virgins (Matthew 25). They were all virgins, all ten of them, but five were foolish and five were wise. All of them had oil at a certain point in time. Later on when it really mattered some of them didn't have oil. Perhaps the year before they were all zealous and anointed with oil. But at the end of it all, some of them had dropped away.

I am teaching on these symptoms and signs of backsliding, because many Christians display these symptoms. If you detect any of these symptoms in yourself, know that you may be on a dangerous path to destruction.

Let's read on.

Bad Company

Experience in the ministry has taught me to take note of any Christian who keeps bad company. It is a very bad symptom, with a very poor prognosis. *Bad* company will eventually lead you to bad places. When you see a Christian who has bad friends, it is likely he will find his way out of church one-day.

Bad company ruins good morals.
1 Corinthians 15:33 (Revised Standard Version)

There is a saying: "Birds of the same feather flock together."

One Ghanaian proverb can be rendered: **"Show me your friend, and I will show you your character."** This means that we can tell the kind of person you are by just looking at the kind of friends you have.

Within every large church there are smaller groups of Christians. When you observe these groups, you will discover that they are people with the same kind of "feather". The friends you move with will either lead you to church or to bad places.

If you are a real believer and you want to remain in Christ, then you need to have good friends. They should be real born-again Christians, who attend a "born-again" church. They must believe the things you believe.

You must go to church together. Your friends must not have anything against your going to church. If they do, they must not be your friends!

"Do" Them Before They "Do" You

If you keep bad friends they will eventually convert you, or you will convert them. We had this saying in my school, (Achimota School) **"Do them before they do you."** This is a warning to influence your friends before they influence you!

The way to deal with bad company is to convert them and bring them to Christ, before they cause you to backslide.

This, you must realize, requires a lot of wisdom and if you are not a stable Christian yourself, don't attempt converting your bad friends - you may fall away!

Can Your Wife Be Bad Company?

Some people do not realise that the person they marry will keep them company for the rest of their lives, and this 'marital company' will truly affect you.

This is how King Solomon, who built the temple and accomplished great things for the Lord, eventually backslid. The Bible tells us that his wives turned his heart away from God. **Solomon's wives were bad company for him.**

You do not need to expose yourself to the circumstances of bad company. You are not more anointed than Solomon. If the Bible warns that bad company can ruin your life, you'd better believe it and save yourself!

Every wife affects her husband, and every husband has great influence over his wife. Whoever you are, your wife will influence the way you think. If your husband thinks in a certain way, in the process of time, you will eventually think in the same way.

I remember a sweet old lady who had nothing against other races. However, after being married for many years to a racist, she became prejudiced herself.

If your wife does not want you to be in the ministry, you will not be in the ministry. I know this from experience. If my wife had opposed my going into the ministry, I don't think I would have been able to come this far. That is why I am very concerned about who my pastors get married to.

Bad company - whether friends, brothers, husbands, or wives - will lead to backsliding.

Stay clear!

Looking Backwards

In Genesis 19, we can study the testimony of Lot and his wife. Two angels were sent to Lot and his family in Sodom and Gomorrah. Their message was simple:

...Escape for thy life, LOOK NOT BEHIND THEE... lest thou be consumed.

Genesis 19:17

But the Bible declares that Lot's wife looked back and became a pillar of salt.

Jesus also reminds us of the terrible mistake that Lot's wife made as she was escaping from Sodom and Gomorrah.

She was the only member of the family who looked back at her past. We can liken this to believers who backslid because they kept looking back at the world and all it had to offer.

As born-again believers, God has delivered all of us from sin, and it is important that we do not look back.

I Went out with Many Men

I always remember the story of a lady who stood before a Christian group to testify. She happily recounted what she had done as an unbeliever:

"I used to go out with many men. They would pick me up to party with me at nightclubs and discos. I danced all night with them. It was great." She said.

With great excitement in her voice, she told the Christians: "I traveled all over the world with them. We really had a good time."

Then her voice dropped and she sadly said, "But I got saved, and here I am in church."

To her, salvation was rather the 'bad' thing that happened to her. It was as though being saved was an unfortunate experience. This woman was looking back to the expensive cars, the chinese restaurants and the "good" times she had had as an unbeliever. **If you keep on thinking and remembering your past sinful life with nostalgia, you will turn into "a pillar of salt"!**

When you see a married woman who talks with excitement about her past boyfriends, then you are looking at a woman who may not be happy where she is.

It is most probable that she may want to go back to her "great" guys.

You will go back if you keep looking back. And you will fall if you keep looking backwards.

I am looking ahead, and I intend to go forward with God's work. As a medical doctor in full-time ministry, I could look back and consider returning to the practice of medicine.

There are times when I can remember the peculiar smell of the hospital. I remember those days when I walked the wards and heard the patients call, "Dr. Mills", "Please, Dr. Mills." But I am not looking back. **I am going forward, preaching, teaching and planting churches all over the world.** I have no intention of going back to the full-time practice of medicine.

If there is a longing in your heart to *go backwards* or to *look backwards,* then you are manifesting a dangerous symptom of backsliding. Come before the Lord and ask Him to help you "kill" that interest in the past. Let it die!

Over-Confidence

An over-confident person is someone who has too much trust in his abilities. It is dangerous to be over-confident as a Christian. Being too confident in your righteousness and in your own spirituality is a bad sign.

...Let him that THINKETH HE STANDETH take heed lest he fall.
1 Corinthians 10:12

If you regard yourself or your position in Christ as foolproof, you are in danger of backsliding - especially, if you have had promotion in church, or have been used by God in the past.

I have heard some Christians boast, "I will never fornicate, I cannot simply do it." - this is over-confidence. It reminds me of a particular brother in my church who would regularly come to me and say: "Pastor, your church is so good, I will never leave Lighthouse Chapel."

He spoke about his commitment to me and to the church with such conviction. A few months later, he walked out of the church and never returned.

Satan Smiles at Boasting Christians

When a Christian continues to boast about his strength, Satan hears him and decides to test him. Such a person is a potential backslider.

Where you are over-confident is where you can be the weakest, because you have dropped your guard.

You can also tell that a Christian is over-confident by the way he talks about the weaknesses of others. I have heard Christians criticize others as though they could never make the same mistakes. They overestimate their own ability, and look down on others.

Do Not Laugh at Them

You need to be humble, otherwise one day you will find yourself in the same shoes, much to your own surprise. Staying on the right track is largely by the grace of God, and not by your own strength.

When David heard that Saul was dead, he didn't ridicule him or rejoice over his death. David could have lashed out at Saul and criticized him at that time. He could have taken the opportunity to talk about how Saul had been disobedient and stubborn. He could have discussed what led to Saul's downfall. Instead he declared,

Tell it not in Gath, publish it not in the streets of Askelon...

2 Samuel 1:20

Although David did not have a problem with stubbornness and disobedience, he did not venture to denounce his predecessor because of his weaknesses. We must all learn something from this example.

47

...Let him that THINKETH HE STANDETH TAKE HEED lest he fall.

1 Corinthians 10:12

Stubbornness

The next symptom of backsliding is stubbornness. A stubborn person is prone to falling away.

The backslider in heart shall be filled with his own ways...

Proverbs 14:14

If you know a stubborn Christian who does not heed counsel, but will always do what he wants to do in spite of all advice, you are looking at a potential backslider.

And my people are BENT TO BACKSLIDING from me...

Hosea 11:7

Often I would counsel Christians and find at the end of the session that they are still set in their ways. They are bent on doing their own thing. Everybody needs advice. The Bible says there is safety in the multitude of counsel.

Better is a poor and a wise child than an old and foolish king, who will no more be admonished.

Ecclesiastes 4:13

I remember counselling a young lady not to continue in a certain unhealthy relationship.

Are You Different From the Other Girls?

I asked, "What makes you different from the other girls he has thrown away? He has had 17 girlfriends, and you are the 18th. The only difference between you and the others is that you are new to him. But one day you will become 'old' just like the others. And he will then throw you away." Inspite of this admonition, she persisted in her ways.

Is there anybody who was mightily blessed by God although he was stubborn and rebellious? Never! **Stubbornness to God, to His Word, to His pastors and to biblical counsel is a sign that backsliding is imminent.**

Christian Surprises

There is something I call *"Christian surprises"*. "Christian surprises" are surprises that are unique to the Christian experience. **These are shocks you experience in the course of your Christian walk.** Unfortunately, some people get so shocked by what they see and hear in church that it actually makes them fall away.

As we grow as Christians, we will encounter these Christian surprises. Most of us are quite naïve when we become Christians. We think we have come into a perfect world.

So, when the so-called born-again saints disappoint us we become so amazed. We can't believe it's true. But the Bible says we should not be amazed. A shocked or amazed Christian can easily fall away from the faith.

> **...as long as ye do well, and are not afraid with any AMAZEMENT.**
>
> **1 Peter 3:6**

> **...and let nothing terrify you - not giving way to hysterical fears or letting anxieties unnerve you.**
>
> **1 Peter 3:6 (Amplified Bible)**

Being in a state of shock is being in a dangerous condition. Any good doctor who sees a patient in a state of shock knows that he is dealing with someone who can easily pop off and die.

Any experienced pastor who sees his members in a state of shock and surprise at what may have happened in the church also knows that he is looking at a member who can easily fall away.

All Leaders Are Human!

One of the things that may cause Christians to fall away is disappointment in a Christian leader. Sometimes your leader can disappoint you beyond measure. Samson, David, Peter and other mighty leaders made mistakes. That could have disappointed their followers, and caused them to backslide.

The Bible tells pastors not to be greedy, pompous or lord their authority over others. It states clearly that pastors should not run after money, or women. God's ministers are supposed to do His work from their hearts.

The very fact that the Bible speaks about all of these things means that Christian leaders *can* do them (and *have* done them)!

These days one of the favourite activities of the press is to write stories about fallen men of God.

Some pastors have been involved in sex, money and breakaway scandals.

Christians have been surprised at such behavior coming from the people they have loved and looked up to for many years. Such surprising behavior often destabilizes hitherto 'stable' believers. But remember the Word of God.

... there is no new thing under the sun. Is there anything whereof it may be said, See this is new? it hath been already of old time...

Ecclesiastes 1:9, 10

If you have all through your Christian life, put your trust in a man, then it is very likely that you will be disappointed.

Fix Your Eyes on Jesus

Paul said, "Follow me as I follow Christ." Which means you can only follow your Christian leader as long as he follows Christ! **I often tell my church, "The day I stop following Christ, is the day you stop following me".**

I remember when some great men of God in the United States fell into sin, many Christians also fell away from the faith with them. Why was this so? They had experienced a Christian surprise. But they needn't have fallen. **If you fix your eyes on Christ** (looking unto Jesus)**, you will be a stable Christian.**

Christians may also become surprised when they pray, but do not get the answers they expect. A close member of the family may be terminally ill, or you may have been praying for your husband to be saved, only to see him get worse. You can easily feel surprised and shocked that God has ignored your prayers.

Do not be surprised! It is not everything that you know. I hope you know *that!* **You are still learning, and you are still growing in the Lord.**

I Was Surprised!

I remember one time when I was travelling to Tamale, a town in the northern part of Ghana. I was driving with the pastors of our branches in Kumasi, Zurich and a Canadian trainee pastor. On the highway, two bicycle riders suddenly crossed my path.

I had to apply the brakes immediately in order to avoid hitting them. When I did this, my car began to skid, and before I could say 'Jack Robinson', we were somersaulting in the air. The car eventually rolled to a halt some 30 metres off the road. We were now literally upside down, with the wheels of the car in the air!

When we all came out alive and well, I must admit that I was surprised - and almost angry with God. Why should God allow such a thing to happen to us? Didn't He know that we were all pastors travelling only to do more of His work?

However, a few days later the Spirit of God ministered certain things to me privately.

One thing I can tell you that He said to me was, "Instead of being angry and surprised, you should be grateful that I have allowed this to happen in order to draw your attention to something very important for your life and ministry".

You may not understand this now, but as you grow in Christ you will understand it better by and by.

Surprisingly, Jesus Did Not Heal Everyone!

When Jesus was here, He did not heal everybody. Jesus went to the pool of Bethsaida, a place that had a host of sick people. (That is the equivalent of a modern hospital.)

But he only healed one man, who had been sick for 38 years.

Why didn't He heal any of the others? Jesus said, "My Father works, and I work". Jesus meant that he was doing exactly what His Father was doing. Should we be surprised at this move of Christ? **We have to learn to trust in the Sovereignty of God and not be annoyed with Him**.

The Disciples Were Surprised!

The arrest and crucifixion of Christ *surprised* the disciples. A week before He had sat on a donkey, and the crowds had cheered Him. They hailed and sang, "Hosanna, blessed is He that comes in the name of the Lord!"

The disciples knew that He was a great man. But a week later he was killed on the cross like a common criminal.

They must have been very surprised. As we all know, these frightened, surprised and disappointed disciples deserted their Saviour and were scattered . This is the equivalent of backsliding.

I Try Not to Be Surprised

Ever since I became a pastor, the lifestyles, habits and practices of some Christian leaders have surprised me. But I have had to teach myself not to be surprised anymore. What has been even more bewildering is the *duality* of some ministers. I remember one minister who spoke of committing fornication almost as if it was an everyday occurrence in his life. Yet this man was the pastor of a church. Time and time again, I have had to brace myself and decide not to be astonished or amazed by what goes on around me. Otherwise I may have left the Ministry by now!

Decide not to be surprised, astonished, dazed, bewildered, or even angry with some of the things you see in Christianity. Keep your focus on Christ and His Word.

To Be Easily Offended

When you see someone who is very touchy, easily hurt and offended, you are looking at a potential backslider.

I remember one absentee church member whom we visited. We wanted to know why she was not in church anymore.

She told us that once, when she came in late, the ushers wrongly seated her and later relocated her. This had

happened more than once. So she became offended and decided not to come to church anymore. This person was offended by the inexperienced usher and simply left the church. Imagine that!

Some church members are irritated because the pastor does not seem to remember their names. Others are offended because the pastor did not say hello when he met them in town. Think about this for a moment; why would the pastor deliberately not say hello to his own church member? Does it make sense? Is he trying to gather people or to scatter and offend them? Could it not be that the pastor didn't recognize you, or that he genuinely did not notice you? Think about it!

A Touchy Person Is Difficult to Live with

If you marry a touchy person, you will always have problems. They are the ones who complain, "Why didn't you smile today? I put my toothbrush in the center, why have you moved it to the right? How come the towel is wet? Don't leave my towel on the bed. Why have you put my shoes here instead of there?" It's very difficult to live with people like that. They are not only difficult marriage partners, but also difficult church

53

members for the pastor. They can even become offended with God Himself!

My Father Died Whilst I Prayed

If I were to be easily offended, I would not have been able to continue in the ministry. Some years ago, I travelled from Ghana to start a church in Zurich. While I was fasting and praying to establish God's work, my father died back home in Ghana.

Throughout the week before he died, he had been seriously ill, but I wasn't fully informed about what was going on. Then one day after I had been praying and fasting for 5 days and nights, my father died about 11 O'clock in the morning.

One of my associate pastors called to inform me about what had happened. I was shocked and surprised. And when I put the phone down, I wept like a baby.

I had every reason to be offended with God. Wasn't I on the mission field, doing *His* work? I consoled myself that I would understand it better by and by and truly, I have not become disillusioned with the ministry. I am pressing on!

If a Christian easily gets hurt, he is likely to backslide!

CHAPTER 6

More Symptoms...

Forgetfulness

God warned the children of Israel:...AND THOU FORGET the Lord...which brought thee forth...
Deuteronomy 8:14

Christians fall away from Christ because they forget where they came from. They forget that their source is Christ. Don't ever forget that it is Christ who brought you to your position, and blessed you.

Don't Forget Where You Are Coming from

Many of us have forgotten who we used to be. We have forgotten what it was like to have a hangover in the morning.

We have forgotten what it was like to have your different girlfriends "clashing". We have forgotten the fear of not knowing whether you have contracted gonorrhoea or AIDS.

Let us remember where the Lord brought us from. When we bought our first church building, we were all so excited. We marched from the Korle-Bu Hospital in Accra, to our new headquarters location, amidst singing and dancing. The building was an old cinema that we rebuilt into a beautiful cathedral. Indeed, we played before the Lord.

Somebody who watched me later on video laughed and commented: "It seems that old cinema hall meant a lot to you". I replied, "You don't know where the Lord has brought me from. I have not forgotten, and I do not intend to forget."

Many churches have forgotten the vision and principles of their founders. They have forgotten the ideals and standards which their founding fathers stood for. That is why many of them are in a backslidden condition. **If some founders of churches were to rise from the dead now, I believe that many of them would not join the very churches they founded. The current leaders would even reject them.**

I always try to remember why I came into the ministry. Why did I leave the respected and noble practice of medicine to come into the often controversial and ridiculed job of being a pastor?

My original motivation was to win souls. I keep that at the forefront of my mind and I keep pressing on to win more souls. If I forget that, I can easily slide into education, medicine, social work or even politics. Anybody who forgets can slip and slide into things he didn't intend to involve himself with.

Not Fasting

Fasting keeps the believer from backsliding. In the Bible the word associated with fasting is *affliction*. In fact, the word affliction can be interchanged for fasting.

Wherefore have we FASTED...wherefore have we AFFLICTED our soul...

Isaiah 58:3

Be AFFLICTED, and mourn, and weep...

James 4:9

Before I was AFFLICTED I went astray: but now have I kept thy word.

Psalm 119:67

How do you afflict yourself? According to the psalmist, one way you can afflict yourself is by fasting.

Fasting Keeps You on Track!

He said that before he fasted he went astray, but when he fasted, he was able to keep God's Word and stay on track.

Then in Psalm 119:71, he says, "It is good for me that I have been afflicted, that I might learn thy statutes." Do you think that God is saying it is good to have sickness and disease? Affliction in that sense is not sickness. In this context God is saying that it is good for the Christian to fast.

Fasting Makes You Humble!

Another word that is associated with fasting is humility. In James 4:10, the Word of God says, "Humble yourself in the sight of God and He will lift you up." When the psalmist fasted in Psalm 35:13, he said, "I humbled my soul with fasting".

Carrying your pastor's bible, speaking softly, or walking slowly are *not* signs of humility. God says you can humble yourself by fasting.

During a fast, especially when you have not eaten for several days, you experience extreme weakness in your body. This kind of suffering in the flesh sobers you. It makes you humble. And if there is anything we need in this modern age of christianity, it is humility. **Remember that pride comes before a fall, and fasting will take away the pride that leads many to a fall.**

As a believer you need to fast, otherwise your flesh will dominate you, and lead you into fleshly sins. To be carnally minded is death.

Some Problems Will Be Solved Only When You Fast

Another reason for fasting is that there are particular problems that can only be solved through fasting. Some people have problems that are going to make them backslide.

Some of these problems that cause backsliding must be solved through fasting. Jesus told his disciples after they failed to heal an epileptic,

...THIS KIND goeth not out but by prayer and FASTING.

Matthew 17:21

Jesus meant here that not all problems are the same. Some difficult ones can be solved only through fasting. It is no wonder that Christians who do not fast are weighed down by all kinds of problems.

Even winter should not prevent Christians from fasting. I have heard Christians in Europe and America complain that it is not possible to fast during the winter. *It is possible.*

During several of my church-planting exercises, I have had to fast during the winter.

I remember once when a brother visited and realized I was fasting, he could not believe it. He asked me, "How can you fast when it is so cold?" He explained that eating helps to keep warm.

Fasting Prevents Spiritual Coldness

But this is the very reason why many African Christians who live in Europe and America are a far cry from what they used to be in their own countries. They have stopped fasting for various reasons, and have grown spiritually cold.

Fasting is not an option. Jesus said in Matthew 6:16: "when ye fast…" He didn't say *if* you fast. This means He expects us to fast.

Fasting has its rewards. In Isaiah 58, God has listed some of the rewards of fasting.

Then shall thy light break forth as the morning, and thine HEALTH shall spring forth speedily… Then shalt thou call, and the Lord shall answer: thou shalt cry, and he shall say, Here I am...

Isaiah 58:8, 9

One of the rewards of fasting is that you will stay spiritually healthy.

Fasting Less

The next symptom of a person who is backsliding is the symptom of fasting less. Fasting is a spiritual exercise that keeps us on our toes. **The more you fast, the more spiritual energy you generate. The more you fast, the more spiritually tuned up you will be.** If you used to fast regularly sometime ago, but now fast less, it is a possible sign that you are becoming "cold".

Fasting Is Not an Option

The prophet Daniel was eighty years old when he fasted for three weeks. Even pregnancy should not make a Christian woman abandon her fasting life. During pregnancy, you should be able to fast to some extent, and still remain healthy. 'The baby may become anointed and grow even better'.

Fasting less is a sign that your investment into spiritual things is gradually decreasing.

Anger at Correction

Any believer who gets angry at correction must be watched closely.

Reprove not a scorner, lest he hate thee: rebuke a wise man, and he will love thee.

Proverbs 9:8

A wise man will be happy at correction because he will think through it and realize that he is being helped. **Often the truth is painful.** When Jesus told the crowd in John 8:44 "…ye are of your father the devil…" they were offended.

Jesus Called Peter Satan

On one occasion, Jesus addressed Peter and said to him, "Get thee behind me, *Satan.*" Notice that Peter was not angry at being called Satan. After this rebuke, Peter went on to become the great man of God who preached to thousands!

A friend at school told someone who was irritating him, "Satan, get thee behind me." This person was *astonished, amazed* and *very offended* at being called "Satan". His reaction was very different from Peter's!

I have never referred to anybody as Satan (although I have seen many people behave just like the devil). I wonder what would happen if I dared to correct someone by referring to him as Satan? He would probably explode in anger!

The Musician Was Not Offended

During a visit to one of my branch churches, an instrumentalist was very rude to his choir director. The pastor in charge sternly rebuked this musician. I watched this scene quietly from the side, wondering what would happen next.

Fortunately this musician did not get angry at his pastor's rebuke and is doing well up until today. I know some musicians who would have walked out at that kind of correction.

Better is a poor and a wise child than an old and foolish king, who will no more be admonished.

Ecclesiastes 4:13

A Good Father Will Correct You

God gave us fathers and mothers to correct and advise us. You should thank God if your parents are alive.

There are many people who do not have strong fathers to guide them. Such people often go astray. My wife tells me that she wanted to be a secretary for the wrong reasons, but her father counseled her. He encouraged her to study law. Today she is glad that she followed her father's advice and became a lawyer.

Those who do not have good parents to guide and correct them are at a disadvantage. **Correction will help you stay on track, so do not be angry at correction!**

Allowing the Cares of the World to Choke the Word

And the cares of this world...choke the word, and it becometh unfruitful.

Mark 4:19

Jesus told the story of a sower who went out to sow. Some seeds fell on the wayside, some on stony ground, some amongthorns and the rest on good ground.

Jesus compared the four types of ground to four types of hearts. In one heart, thorns choked the word. In another, the heart was like a stone, so that the Word could not enter. In another heart, the Word fell by the wayside.

Only 25% of the Seeds Will Survive

It was only the good heart that bore fruit. **This story implies that only about a quarter of all those who hear the Word of God will eventually remain in Christ and be fruitful.**

What are the cares of the world? Paying your debts, your bills, and all the responsibilities that go with family life fall under these "cares".

There is nothing wrong with paying your bills or looking after your family. Indeed, if you have a wife or family, you ought to look after them. A husband's duty is to fellowship with his wife and take care of his children. These are legitimate challenges that every one in this world will have to grapple with.

God warns us against becoming over burdened with these responsibilities. These cares should not dominate our lives. **When they begin to dominate your life, you are in danger of backsliding.**

As a pastor, I have observed that when Christians take on new jobs, they become so engrossed in them - to the detriment of their spiritual lives. Sometimes because of such new jobs, they neither go to church nor have their quiet times any more. The cares of the world have begun to cause backsliding.

Every student's 'care' is to pass his examinations but God should not be excluded from your life because of your books.

As a medical student I successfully combined my schoolwork with my pastoral work. For years I was a student as well as a pastor. I have never put the Word or the work of God aside because of school.

In my ministry, I have had medical students pastoring large branches of the church faithfully. It is not an impossible task.

As a medical student, I often asked, "Is being a medical student a curse? Does it mean that I cannot serve God anymore? Does it mean I have to backslide?" The answer is no! Being a medical student is just another 'care' of this world which must not be allowed to choke God's Word and work.

Don't Backslide Because You Are Pregnant

A new baby or a pregnancy should not make you backslide. Other Christians have made it, and so can you!

When our first son was born, I carried him to church when he was only **seven days** old. I had a preaching appointment to honour, and had to go with my wife and my newborn son. I remember how we carried our seven-day-old baby through the cold weather onto the buses, and in the streets in order to keep this preaching appointment in Geneva.

My baby didn't die. Neither will yours, if you continue to do the work of the Lord. I am sorry to say that many new mothers are backsliding Christians, because they are allowing the cares of the world to choke their Christian lives.

Allowing Riches to Choke the Word

...and the deceitfulness of riches,...choke the word, and it becometh unfruitful.

Mark 4:19

Those who are very rich have certain problems which poorer people do not have. These problems of the rich tend to keep them away from church.

When we first purchased the Lighthouse Cathedral property, we ran into a new problem which we did not have before. We had to think of security! We hadn't thought of security before, because we had never had any property to protect.

I have noticed that as people become more successful they tend to stay away from church. When the Lord blesses you, do not make the mistake of allowing the responsibilities associated with new blessings to choke the Word.

Remember that it was God who gave you the power to acquire wealth. **God, by blessing you, did not intend to keep you away from Him!**

You rarely see the so-called "big-shots" at prayer meetings and crusades. They do not turn up for all night prayer meetings probably because they are tired from all the work they do, or because the time could be spent doing something "profitable"!

Learn how to maintain the glow inspite of your newfound treasures. Don't allow your riches to crowd out the Lord.

The Lust of the World

...and the lusts of other things entering in, choke the word, and it becometh unfruitful.

Mark 4:19

Lust for anything apart from God's Word is dangerous. It can ruin your life because you will sacrifice so many things to get what you want.

There are Christians who will sacrifice anything to ride in a mercedes benz. They will steal, cheat and lie to own one. Such Believers have a strong desire to have some material possession, and they will do all they can to have it.

This strong *overpowering desire* is what God calls lust. But lust is dangerous! It destroys.

...having escaped the CORRUPTION that is in the world through LUST.

2 Peter 1:4

Corruption has come into the world through lust.

Governments are often corrupt because of officials who have strong desires to acquire certain possessions. These officials take bribes in exchange for illegal favours.

They also receive gifts and handouts in exchange for signing bogus contracts which ruin the economies of entire nations. **Lust** (strong desires) **corrupts people.**

Desire the Will of God

As a minister I have learnt not to have a strong desire for anything in particular. It can easily destroy your ministry. Mind you, I also have desires, but they are subject to the Word of God in me. The strongest desire in a Christian's life should be for the will of God to prevail.

> **...Take heed, and beware of covetousness: for a man's life consisteth not in the abundance of the things which he possesseth.**
>
> **Luke 12:15**

There is *nothing* that is worth sacrificing your Christianity for. You will only live (or die) to regret it. **If you see someone who has a very strong desire for material things, you are looking at a potential backslider.** One day the devil will dangle that thing in front of you, and you may just walk out on Christ to get it.

Some Christians desperately want a husband, and therefore they will break all the rules, and sacrifice every moral principle in order to get one. Others desperately want to have a child. And they will go as far as having sex with other men if their husbands are sterile.

He Said, "I Don't Trust Any Woman."

Once when I was working in the hospital, a doctor friend explained that his work in the gynecological department had made him distrust women.

He said he had seen female patients whom, when they realized their husbands were sterile, went ahead and sacrificed their marital vows in order to become pregnant. He related how one husband had come to his house weeping for joy after his wife had had a baby.

He marvelled, "This man did not know that his wife had cheated on him and had had a child by another man." Do not let your craving for material possessions make you backslide.

A Poor Quality Conscience

A person who does not have a good conscience is a potential backslider. A good conscience is necessary to keep you on track. It is the next symptom of backsliding I want us to consider.

Holding faith, and A GOOD CONSCIENCE; which some having put away concerning faith have made shipwreck: Of whom is Hymenaeus and Alexander; whom I have delivered unto Satan, that they may learn not to blaspheme.

1 Timothy 1:19-20

Two church members, Hymenaeus and Alexander, put away faith and a *good conscience*, and thus, they made shipwreck of their Christian lives. As long as we put our conscience away, we will have the capacity to do greater and greater evil until the day that we forsake God.

Your Conscience Is a Voice - Protect it!

The conscience is the voice of that better component of a human being (whether a Christian or non-christian). **It is the conscience of a man that tries to keep him from doing evil.** It is important to have a good and strong conscience (inner voice). You can either have a strong conscience or a weak one.

Paul, the great apostle, said he had a good conscience. He also revealed that he had always maintained a good conscience, *even* as an unbeliever.

I dare say that some unbelievers have better consciences than some Christians.

When our conscience becomes hardened, it is difficult for God to speak to us. I have always tried to have a good conscience, because I know the danger of a hardened conscience.

It is this conscience which pricks me everyday and keeps me from backsliding.

When your conscience is gone, that element within you that can stop the backsliding process is also gone. You are no longer touched by the anointing, by the Word of God, by the preaching, or by the Holy Ghost.

Your conscience is like the palm of your hand. Some of us have soft hands, whilst others have callous ones. Your hands will become hardened, and the softness will go away as you do hard work with your hands. **In the same way, your conscience will become hardened as you continue to sin without repenting.**

When believers become indifferent to the promptings of God, it is a dangerous sign.

No Preacher Could Reach Him

A pastor friend of mine whose entire family is saved except for one brother told me his story. He related how his mother had taken his brother to so many Full Gospel Breakfast meetings that he had become hardened.

He had heard many different testimonies from several speakers but these no longer made an impact on his life. Indeed, he knew when the speaker would make an altar call. He knew what the next item on the programme was.

Many Christians can lie and their consciences will not prick them anymore. Some of them can even invent false stories without batting an eyelid.

I have heard of pastors who say they preach best after fornicating. The difference between these pastors and you is just a gradual process of hardening. You become harder and harder as you become used to sin. Then at a point when you sin you won't be bothered anymore.

You can commit bigger or smaller sins depending on your conscience. If you have a very sensitive conscience, the sins that you can commit will be 'small' ones. But as your conscience becomes more hardened and more worn out, your ability to commit 'wilder' sins grows.

I Don't Care if I Go to Heaven or Hell

Recently, I sat before a certain rich man, and I said to him, "You must be prepared to meet your God at anytime." He was with two of his wealthy friends. He replied that he was not prepared, but he really didn't care.

When you get to the stage where you don't care whether you go to heaven or hell, then you are in danger. Perhaps, when you were younger you would have cared, but now, you are so hardened that you don't care anymore.

Every Christian needs to have a sensitive conscience. Do not get used to sin. Do not get to the stage where you do not care anymore. **Be sensitive to the little promptings of the inner voice, so you don't backslide!**

CHAPTER 7

Even More Symptoms...

Praying Less

The next symptom of backsliding I want us to consider is praying less. Jesus said, "Pray lest you fall into temptation".

Prayer keeps us from falling away from God. Anybody you spend time talking to becomes close to you. In the same way, any Christian who spends time talking to God will become close to Him. **It follows that if you don't spend time praying to God, you will be far from Him.**

This is one of the principles that explain how people can have extra-marital affairs. Many of us forget that if you continuously communicate with somebody, he or she becomes close to you.

You can unknowingly fall in love with a man or woman who is not your partner.

Spending time together with somebody makes you close, whether you intend to be close or not. So when a Christian spends less time praying, he is unknowingly moving away from God.

The Day I Met a *Strange Woman*

When you pray, God gives you strength to overcome temptations. He will strengthen you to do His will and you will not fall away. Many years ago, God knew I was going to experience a serious testing of my Christian faith so He woke me up early in the morning to pray.

Tongues were flowing out of my spirit like a river and I knew something was amiss, so I prayed the more. I laid down on the floor and continued in prayer. As a young Christian I was normally doing an hour a day in prayer, but this time I prayed for over three hours. And that day I met a strange woman.

The Bible tells us about a young man in Proverbs who met a strange woman. I had a similar experience.

And, behold, there met him a woman with the attire of an harlot, and subtil of heart.

Proverbs 7:10

I had no idea what this Christian lady had in mind. But that day, I tell you my friend, God delivered me! I believe my deliverance was very much related to the prayer time I had had in the morning. I was very strong. Where did that strength come from? Jesus told His disciples to pray because they might fall into temptation.

The Lord gave me strength through prayer. **If you see a Christian who doesn't pray, you are looking at a Christian who will fall into one temptation after another, until he eventually backslides.**

Not Being Committed

The next symptom of backsliding I want us to consider is the symptom of not being committed. Anybody who does not want to be committed to a church, will ultimately leave that church.

There are countless Christians who are just visiting churches, but are not committed to any of them. These are the 'watching Christians'. They are watching out for how things will turn out by the next month. If they don't feel too happy with the pastor or his sermons, they will move to the next church.

God expects the believer to be like a tree that is *planted* by the rivers of water. The rivers of water are the powerful, life-changing messages that flow from the pulpit every Sunday. Every Christian must be planted in the house of the Lord. **You must have somebody to relate to as your pastor. God created us in a special way so that we are like sheep, who need a shepherd.** You need to belong somewhere!

I remember one friend who finally came home after sojourning in Europe for sometime. He didn't want to join this church, or that church. He was just not committed anywhere. He would go here today and there tomorrow. **At a point I had to remind him that it is only the devil who goes to and fro according to the Book of Job! An uncommitted Christian is a potential backslider.**

Irregular Fellowship

The next symptom is the symptom of having irregular fellowship. I think this is one of the most important symptoms. It is actually one of the *most common.*

Your heart is supposed to beat at regular intervals. But unfortunately, some people have an irregular heartbeat. This means that when their hearts beat correctly once or twice, it is followed by a mis-timed beat. An irregular heartbeat may be *regularly* irregular or *irregularly* irregular. Please try and understand what I am saying.

Are You Irregularly Irregular?

A patient with an *irregularly* irregular heartbeat is suffering from what is called atrial fibrillation and experiences symptoms like fainting and palpitations.

To prevent death such people's hearts need to be stabilized.

Unfortunately, there are many Christians who have this problem of being irregular in their spiritual walk. This irregularity is either *regular* or *irregular*. Their church attendance may be regularly (constantly) irregular. (For instance they *constantly* come to church once or twice a month).

For some, church attendance may be irregularly irregular. For such people their church attendance may be *totally unpredictable* throughout the year. The pastor cannot predict when they will next be in church. **Can you imagine what it would be like if you didn't know when next your heart would beat?**

Television and radio sermons cannot substitute regular fellowship. You must have a specific church, which you attend regularly. Observe the irregular Christians. You will notice how they tend to backslide. But the regular feeding of your spirit will keep you from backsliding.

Laziness and Excuses

The next symptom you must watch out for is laziness and excuses

The slothful man saith, There is a lion without, I shall be slain in the streets.

Proverbs 22:13

The lazy Christian is full of amazing excuses. He would say he couldn't leave his bed because of an imaginary lion in the street. **Such a person will not amount to much because anyone who wants to be successful must be prepared to work hard!**

Hard Work Breeds Success

When I was in Achimota school I passed with distinction at the ordinary level exams. It didn't just happen. I had to work very hard. While some of the students were playing around, I was studying very hard.

In the third year of my medical schooling I earned another distinction. In preparation for that exam, I didn't sleep in the night for six weeks. I slept in the afternoons between 2p.m. and 6p.m. Then from 6p.m. till the next day at 2p.m., I wouldn't sleep. I would go for walks, memorizing and retaining some of the course material.

I remember walking up and down in the 'R' Block of the medical students' hostel, memorizing all sorts of information about worms, flies, and insects: this worm lays so many eggs per minute, that insect flies at this speed per second, it dives at this angle into the water, etc.

When other students were asleep, I was walking behind their rooms memorizing things about worms, crabs, scorpions and every other creature I had to learn about.

When you see somebody succeeding as a Christian, or doing well in any sphere, he must be working hard!

Seest thou a man diligent in his business? he shall stand before kings; he shall not stand before mean men.
Proverbs 22:29

All those who are doing well are not magically blessed; their success comes out of working very hard. In the same way, those who are not backsliding are not just miraculously staying on course. They are working hard at their Christian lives!

The Lighthouse Chapel International is doing well because so many different people contribute towards church growth. There are pastors who work very hard and often leave the church premises very late. There are also unpaid volunteers who make great sacrifices of time. It is this great commitment that makes the church work.

Laziness will not take anybody to Heaven. *Seest thou a man who is slothful; he can easily go to Hell!* It takes hard work to stay on track with God.

Watch the lazy Christians in the church; they are prone to backsliding!

73

Coldness

Coldness is the next symptom of backsliding I want us to consider.

And because iniquity shall abound, the love of many shall wax COLD.

Matthew 24:12

You can detect coldness by first identifying *"coolness"* in church.

Christian Diplomats

Some Christians are very 'cool' in the house of the Lord. They refuse to be part of jubilant praise and worship. They don't join in shouting or clapping their hands to the Lord.

They just refuse to release themselves in the presence of the Lord. **I call these people "Christian diplomats".** To all such people I say: there is no place for diplomacy in Christianity!

If you want God to be attracted to you, then be like King David. David lost all his inhibitions when he danced before the Lord. There was no coolness about the way he danced. **In fact, he danced until his clothes fell off!**

The backsliding Christian has no joy in expressing himself before the Lord. To him it is a bother to lift up his hands to the Lord, or shout with the voice of triumph. It is amazing that this same 'cool' Christian would lose his 'coolness' when his favorite soccer team is playing. He will shout, scream and clap his hands when a goal is scored.

I have noticed that when Christians are backsliding they first become aloof, diplomatic and uninterested. They yawn, look bored and keep glancing at their watches during the service. These are manifestations of what I call "coldness" or "coolness". Watch out for them; they are sure signs of imminent backsliding.

Foolish Questioning

Foolish questioning is another symptom of backsliding.

But foolish and unlearned questions avoid...they do gender strifes.

2 Timothy 2:23

Someone asked, "Who made God?"

Another person said, "I'll come to church if you can tell me who Cain's wife was" (Referring to Adam and Eve's first son).

The answer to this particular question is very simple. But it is a foolish question anyway. You see, the problem is not who married Cain; the *real* problem is with your backsliding tendency! You now want to find some reason to doubt the authenticity of the Bible!

You Have the Problem

Others would question "Why are the pastors driving nice cars?" Again, the problem is not with the pastor's car or how much the pastors are being paid. **The problem is that you are backsliding and are trying to find some fault with your church.** You desperately need to find a reason to justify your actions.

These are foolish questions, a classic symptom of a backsliding Christian. Of course, I am not against the asking of legitimate questions. But there is a difference between a *genuine* question and a *foolish* question. **Watch out for those who come up with all sorts of criticisms and reviews of the church and its ministers.** They often have a hidden motive.

Having No Spiritual Ambition

Another symptom of backsliding is having no spiritual ambition. As a believer if you don't go forward, you will go backwards. If you don't have in you an ambition to press forward in Christ, you will have a problem.

I have noticed that Christians who have no spiritual ambition have the tendency to grow "cold" and eventually fall away. Paul had a vision to keep pressing on.

...but this one thing I do, forgetting those things which are behind...I PRESS toward the mark for the prize of the high calling...

Philippians 3:13,14

We must forget the good and the bad and press on ahead. We have all had bad and good experiences in our lifetime. But we must forget about them and press forward. Some Christians are hooked on to the past. They tell tales of the great exploits God used them to do in the past.

You cannot just be content with what happened some years ago. What about the present?

What is God using you to do *today?* The time to minister to others is now.

For when for the time ye ought to be teachers, ye have need that one teach you again...

Hebrews 5:12

One thing that has kept me from falling away is my pursuit of spiritual achievements. You must have a spiritual heart, which will propel you to rise up and go ahead to minister to others.

The greatest blessing you can have is to become a blessing yourself. God promised Abraham that He would bless him so much that he would also become a blessing.

I Couldn't Preach

There was a time in my life when I couldn't preach. But I did not stay there. I knelt down before a mature Christian brother and asked him to lay hands on me so I would be able to preach. After that prayer I started preaching. I stood before little groups and began ministering to them.

Maybe you also have the same problem, or you feel very shy to speak in public. Act in faith by speaking the Word with a few people, and you will be surprised at what God can do. It will keep you from backsliding.

A Christian should have the ambition to be useful in God's house. Many people do not wish to be great in God's house. On the contrary, you will be surprised at the number of believers who crave to be millionaires.

They look for all the opportunities to be great in the secular world. However, when it comes to the things of God, they *have no drive.*

I have always wanted to be a preacher. I listened to and watched other preachers minister. I used to go home from the university to watch videos of preaching. I invested both time and money to achieve my goal. That is why I never backslid.

Pastors! Watch the sheep who have no spiritual drive.

Curiosity

The next symptom of backsliding to notice is the symptom of curiosity.

Curiosity Doesn't Only Kill Cats!

Curiosity, they say killed the cat. But in another sense curiosity also kills many Christians. Some Christians have been deceived by the devil into thinking that they are missing something. So they become curious and want to experiment with these forbidden areas.

Some would say, "I haven't tasted alcohol all my life. I want to know what it feels like to be drunk."

Others would say, "I have never used drugs before and I want to know what it feels like to be 'high'." You may only find out what it is like to be mad! You may acquire what we call marijuana-induced schizophrenia.

I was with my boss in a consulting room at the mental hospital one day when a mother brought in her son. This boy had been experimenting with marijuana.

The Psychiatrist took this young boy on a tour of the mental hospital. There were men in little cubicles making various strange noises. There were special places for very wild and mad men. It reminded me of the zoo.

The Psychiatrist warned this young boy that if he continued experimenting with drugs his curiosity would end him up in this "zoo"! I will never forget that tour.

It is this same kind of curiosity, which led the prodigal son out of his father's house to eat with pigs. What couldn't the prodigal son have had at home? He admitted that his own father's servants had more than enough to eat. He was just curious about what was going on out there.

You will notice men with very beautiful and charming wives, who still chase after other women. Some of these men are just curious. They think there is more to discover.

There is nothing new under the sun. There is nothing new to see. Curiosity killed the backslider!

Murmuring

The next symptom of backsliding is murmuring.

Do all things without murmurings and disputings:

Philippians 2:14

Murmuring means to complain, to grumble, to mumble and to criticize. There are Christians who murmur at home, at work and in church. God is against those who murmur. He was especially displeased with the people of Israel when they murmured against Him and Moses. Some complained and nagged so much that they never made it to the Promised Land.

People who murmur and complain never make it to the Promised Land. **In my experience people who murmur and complain often leave their churches and eventually backslide.**

When you complain against someone, it is likely that you are angry with the person or that you don't like that person anymore.

Those who complain against their governments are often angry with their government. In the same way those who murmur against the church are often angry with God and are ready to leave Him.

Mark those who murmur and complain, because they are potential deserters of the ship.

Approval and Admiration of Evil or Wrongdoers

The next very important symptom is "approval and admiration of wrongdoers". People usually become attracted to something before they go for it. In the same way, if you approve of somebody who is doing the wrong thing, then you are likely to want to do the same thing yourself.

God expects the Christian to disapprove of evil. Although Saul was Jonathan's father, Jonathan acknowledged that the King, his father, was wrong in trying to kill David. David had done no wrong, but out of jealousy, Saul attempted to kill him.

Jonathan disassociated himself from what his father was doing and associated himself with the right, which was David. That is what a real Christian must do. You must not approve of what is wrong. You must be bold and say, "This is wrong, and that is right!" "And I stand for what is right."

Woe unto them that call evil good...

Isaiah 5:20

You Become What You Admire

From experience I have noticed that if you praise evil, one day you will also commit the same evil. If someone is a rebel and you approve of the person, one day you may also be a rebel. I watch for people who do not condemn the evil going on around them. The christian should never approve of evil.

...Wherein have we wearied him? When ye say, Every one that doeth evil is good...

Malachi 2:17

Watch out for Christians who do not disapprove of evil; they are probably thinking of doing the same thing one day.

Poor Adaptation Reflexes

...How shall we sing the LORD'S song in a strange land?

Psalm 137:4

The children of Israel hung their harps upon the willows when they encountered their new circumstances. They packed up their instruments of praise because they had been carried away as captives.

Adapt Quickly to Your New Circumstances

Christians who find it difficult to adapt to their new circumstances often backslide in their walk with God. They cannot adapt themselves to their new roles as wives, husbands, mothers, fathers and so on. They are simply unable to adapt themselves to their new jobs, new husbands, new wives, new babies and so on.

Sometimes when a Christian relocates to another city, he changes from being a strong and vibrant Christian to being cold and indifferent. He can not adapt to his new environment.

Why should you turn your back on God because of your new circumstance? Rise up in the name of Jesus! You wanted so much to have a wife, a husband and a job. Now you have it, so adapt quickly to your new circumstance, and do not backslide.

You Can Sing the Lord's Song

The LORD is my strength and song, and is become my salvation.

Psalm 118:14

Notice the relation between "my strength", "my song" and "my salvation".

You cannot separate your song from your strength. Neither can you separate your strength from your salvation. They go together. You need to sing the Lord's song whatever you do and wherever you find yourself.

Dear friend, even if you are married to an unbeliever, don't give up your walk with the Lord.

Marriage Can Affect Your Anointing

I once heard a "bachelor" pastor being challenged. **He was told, "If you are still anointed after you marry, then you are really called of God."** The message was clear! You will have a lot of adapting to do after you get married, otherwise you will backslide!

...and if thou marry...shall have TROUBLE in the flesh...

1 Corinthians 7:28

Nothing comes cheap. It was extremely difficult for me to become a doctor as well as a pastor. When you become a doctor your life changes. Your life becomes totally involved in the condition of your patients. But I had to quickly adapt to my new circumstance in order to continue with the ministry. You can't put the Lord aside just because you have traveled to a new country or to a new school.

The Christian who cannot adapt quickly to his new circumstances is likely to backslide. You must adapt in order to stay alive!

Learn how to identify these things. Do not be ignorant of the devil's devices. Why fall away now that you know the Lord?

God has great plans for you, there is no doubt about it. He has plans to bless you, to prosper you and to increase you in this life. Remember, however, that such blessings are not meant to *draw* you away from God, but to *establish* your faith and confidence in Him.

Do not let the new circumstances which your blessings may bring cause you to backslide. Develop staying power!

CHAPTER 8

My Last Argument

This is my final argument against backsliding. In this chapter you will see in very real terms the folly of backsliding. You will hear the testimonies of real Christians who made it to the very end. You will also hear the last statements of the backslidden and lost souls, and what they said as they approached the gates of Hell. You will see how really terrible backsliding is.

In our walk with God there is a certain line that we must not cross. There is a point of no return. I have heard believers say that they will backslide, but will come back to the Lord after some time. They forget that there may be a point of no return.

The Point of No Return

We will all stand before the presence of God to account for our lives. When that time comes and you are ushered into the presence of God, what will you say?

Will you be ready? Will you have done what God wanted you to do?

A Christian brother was committing fornication when he heard a loud blast. He thought it was the sound of the trumpet heralding the return of Christ. So he jumped out of the bed, but was not caught up to heaven. He was so worried, because he thought that he had been left behind at the rapture. This anxious Christian was overreacting to the honk of a big bus. A backslider lives in fear and uncertainty.

God Wants to Reason with You

Come now, and let us REASON together...

Isaiah 1:18

God is a rational Being, and He wants to reason with you.

Many people think that when you deal with spiritual things you must put aside all reason and stop thinking rationally. But the Bible records that God wants us to reason with Him. If God tells you to reason, then He must be a God who thinks logically and sequentially!

I am going to reason with you and argue with you about backsliding. You could call it *"Arguments for and against backsliding"*.

I will show you certain people who were *happy and full of joy* as they entered into the rest of God. These were Christians who served the Lord and did not fall away.

On the other hand, I will show you what some dying backsliders said as they left this earth. These testimonies alone should make you decide never, never, never to backslide.

The Saints

First, I want you to notice what Bible saints had to say when they were moving from this world to the next.

Apostle Paul

Apostle Paul was in prison when he knew that his time of death was near. He said, **"For to me…to die is gain."** In other words he was happy to be dying. How many people are happy to die? If you are confident of your relationship with God you will not fear death.

Jacob

When the *Patriarch Jacob* was dying in Genesis 49:33, the Bible declares that **after commanding his sons, "…He gathered up his feet into the bed, and yielded up the ghost…"**

What a way to go! He knew that he was going. He had time to instruct his children with confidence. After commanding his sons, he gathered his feet onto the bed and died. You see, the death of the righteous is very different from the death of the wicked. Balaam the prophet said;

…Let me die the death of the righteous…

Numbers 23:10

Now let's study how some ordinary people, after living a life without backsliding went on happily to be with the Lord.

Ignatius

Ignatius lived in 100 AD. He was the Bishop of Antioch, and a personal disciple of John the Apostle. He was sentenced to death, and as he was dying, his last words were, **"I thank thee, oh God, that thou hast honoured me with thy Word, praise God!"**

These were the last words of a man who was sentenced to death by burning at the stake. Some other people would have been screaming, defaecating and salivating. But this man died praising God!

85

Father Polycarp

Father Polycarp, another disciple of John lived during the reign of Emperor Nero. He was also sentenced to death. He was taken to court, and there, he was given an option to either denounce Jesus or be burnt to death. Polycarp suffered much for Christ's sake. The Roman Proconsul commanded him to swear allegiance to Ceasar, saying, "Swear, and I will set thee at liberty; reproach Christ." How courageous and magnificent was Polycarp's reply!

He said, **"Eighty and six years have I now served Christ, and He has never done me the least wrong. How, then, can I blaspheme my King and my Saviour?"**

Further efforts to make him deny his Lord failed, and Polycarp was condemned to be burned at the stake. When the day came for him to be burned alive, those responsible for the burning wanted to nail him to the stake, but he protested: **"Let me alone as I am: for He who has given me strength to endure the fire, will also enable me, without your securing me by nails, to stand without moving in the pile."**

Finally he exclaimed, **"Oh! Lord, Father of the Beloved Son Jesus Christ. I thank thee that thou has allotted me a place among the Martyrs."**

Augustus Montague Toplady

Augustus Montague Toplady (1710-1778), will ever be famous as the author of one of the most evangelical hymns of the Eighteenth Century, "Rock of Ages," which was first published in 1776. During his final illness, Toplady was greatly supported by the consolations of the Gospel.

Near his last, awaking from a sleep, he said:

"Oh, what delights! Who can fathom the joy of the third Heaven? The sky is clear, there is no cloud. Come, Lord Jesus, come quickly!"

He died saying, **"No mortal man can live after the glories which God has manifested to my soul."**

And with those words he went to be with the Lord.

William Shakespeare

William Shakespeare (1564-1616), the world's outstanding figure in literature, of whose life, times and works a whole library of books has been written, lived near his Bible as the numerous quotations from it in his plays and dramas prove.

A Famous Man Knew the Lord

His end came when he was only 52 years old. His last will that was written in the year he died revealed his faith in God.

"I commend my soul into the hands of God my Creator, hoping and assuredly believing, through the only merits of Jesus Christ my Saviour, to be made partaker of life everlasting, and my body to the earth, whereof it is made."

Matthew Henry

Matthew Henry (1662-1714), was the eminent non-conformist theologian who gave the Church the devotional commentary which held a foremost place in its field. He died a week after his settlement in London as pastor of a church in Hackney, but his end was full of confidence in the Saviour's grace.

His last words were: **"A life spent in the service of God, and in communion with Him, is the most comfortable life that any one can lead in this present world."**

John Wesley

John Wesley, the founder of the great Methodist Church said, **"The best of all is, God is with us."** I really love these last words of this great founder.

John Wesley, of whom it has been said that eternity alone will reveal what the world owes to his mighty ministry, was active to the very end. Until the end, he was full of praise, counsel and exhortations.

The Great Founder Dies in Peace

In his last moments with what remaining strength he had, he cried out twice over, in holy triumph:

"The best of all is, God is with us."

The very last word Wesley was heard to articulate was: **"Farewell!"**

Then, without a lingering groan, the evangelist of the highways and by-ways, beloved pastor of thousands, and father of the great Methodist Church, entered into the joy of his Lord.

Notice again, death to the confident Christian- It was a peaceful transition from one world to another!

Adoniram Judson

Adoniram Judson was a missionary to Asia. In fact, the first American missionary to Asia. He went to Burma, wrote and translated the Bible into the Burmese language.

The Departure of Burma's First American Missionary

He also wrote a dictionary for them. When he was dying he said, **"No one ever left this world with brighter hopes or warmer feelings."**

Don't be afraid, death will not surprise me. In spite of what I say, I feel so strong in Him."

This is a man who had strength when most people are weak. Let's all pray for such staying power, that we may all prevail until the very end.

Charles Bridgman

Charles Bridgman died at the age of twelve. As a child he loved to read his Bible and desired spiritual knowledge. Young Charles would often rebuke his brothers if they forgot to thank God at meal times. When he became ill, he was asked whether he would rather live or die, he answered "I desire to die, that I may go to my Saviour."

The Strength of a Little Boy

As his time drew near, his last words were: **"...Into thy hands I commend my soul! Now close mine eyes. Forgive me, father, mother, brother, sister and all the world! Now I am well, my pain is almost gone, my joy is at hand. Lord have mercy upon me. O Lord, receive my soul unto Thee."** How many young boys of today would speak the way this young man spoke?

Robert Bruce

Robert Bruce, one of the most distinguished men of his time, entered the ministry and became prominent in Edinburgh. Scrupulously maintaining the established norms of the church, he exposed himself to much persecution for the truth's sake.

At the time of his death, he called for the family Bible and said to his daughter:

"Cast up to me the eighth chapter of Romans, and set my finger on these words, 'I am persuaded that NEITHER DEATH NOR LIFE ... SHALL BE ABLE TO SEPARATE ME from the love of God which is in Christ Jesus my Lord.'"

Then Bruce said, **"Is my finger on them?"**

"Yes," said his daughter. Then he replied:

"Now God be with you, my children. I have just breakfasted with you, and shall sup with my Lord Jesus this night."

How exciting it must be when you know you are ready! There can be no reason to backslide when you hear these exciting testimonies.

And Many Others

Another dying Christian said, **"How bright the room, how full of angels!"**

Some other Christian said confidently, **"The battle is fought. The battle is fought, and the victory is won."** With those words, he went to be with the Lord.

Alexander II, full of divine faith, exclaimed: **"I am sweeping through the gates, washed in the blood of the Lamb."**

Someone else said, **"I wish I had the power of writing to describe how pleasant it is to die."**

Another one exclaimed, **"Oh! That I could tell what joy I possess. I am full of rapture, the Lord shines with such power upon my soul. He is come, He is come."**

One surviving believer said, **"I shall soon be with Jesus. PERHAPS I AM TOO ANXIOUS!"**

Is It Always Sweet to Die?

Another person said, **"IT IS SWEET TO DIE."** How will you be able to say, "It is sweet to die" when you have backslidden and you know judgement awaits you?

One Christian brother questioned, **"Can this be death? What? It is better than living. TELL THEM I DIED HAPPILY IN JESUS."**

Another one said, **"They sing. The angels sing. IS THIS DYING? NO, IT IS SWEET LIVING."**

One lucky backslider, *Oliver,* a doctor of philosophy, had lived the life of an infidel. But shortly before his death he repented and turned to the Saviour.

His final word was one of deep regret: "Would that I could undo the mischief I have done! I was more ardent to poison men with infidel principles than any Christian is to spread the doctrines of Christ."

The Sinners

Now, let us consider what some backsliders and sinners said as they were dying. The pride and rebellion of these wicked people did not help matters as they approached the gates of hell and accountability. Some of these people were backslidden Christians. They died as frightened, screaming and hopelessly lost souls. The first person I want us to consider in this category is a man called Tom Paine.

Tom Paine

Tom Paine (1737-1809) was considered to be a literary giant.

He wrote "The Age of Reason" and lived during the revivals of John Wesley and George Whitfield. *He lived a life that was against God, and drew people away from God.* I believe that this is one of the people who have made Europe so anti-Christ and atheist in their way of thinking. One person who witnessed his death said, "He is truly to be pitied."

Although he did not believe in God, at the hour of death on his bed he said, **"I would give worlds, if I had them, that 'Age of Reason' had not been published. Oh! Lord help me. Oh! God, what have I done to suffer so much?" Then after that he said, "But there is no God. Yet if there is a God, what will become of me in the world after? If ever the devil had an agent, I have been that one."**

He Was Frightened to Die

When an elderly woman attending him wanted to leave the room, he said, **"Stay with me. For God's sake, I cannot bear to be left alone. For it is hell to be left alone."**

The very last words of Tom Paine were, **"My God, my God why has thou forsaken me?"** And with these words he died. This is the death of the wicked. Utterly helpless and hopeless in the presence of a righteous God!

Voltaire

Whenever I go to Geneva, I cross over into Ferney- Voltaire, a little French village named after a noted infidel *Voltaire (1694-1778).* One night I drove with the pastor of my church in Geneva to look at a statue of this man.

I saw all of the tributes that were written to his name and all of the good works that he was said to have done for the community. But this man also lived and fought against Christianity.

The Man Who Cursed Christ

Notice what this noted French infidel said of Christ our Saviour: **"Curse the wretch!"** How on earth can you gather so much confidence to curse Christ and call Him a wretch?

He once boasted, **"In twenty years, christianity will be no more. My single hand shall destroy the edifice it took twelve apostles to rear."**

These are the people who have laid the foundations for the atheism that is so prevalent in Europe today.

Shortly after his death, the very house in which he printed his foul literature became the depot of the Geneva Bible Society. **The nurse who attended Voltaire said: "For all the wealth in Europe I would not see another infidel die."**

He Was Helpless and Desperate on His Deathbed

The physician, Trochim, who was with Voltaire at his death said that he cried out *most desperately:*

"I am abandoned by God and man! I will give you half of what I am worth if you will give me six month's life. Then I

shall go to hell, and you will go with me. O Christ! O Jesus Christ!"

Notice the desperation and helplessness of this blasphemer as he descended into the abyss. He himself admitted that he was on his way to hell.

My dear Christian friends, let's make no mistakes about the reality of Heaven and hell.

Thomas Hobbes

Thomas Hobbes (1588-1674), was a noted English political philosopher whose most famous work was "Leviathan".

This cultured, clever skeptic corrupted many of the great men of his time. But what regret was his at the end of the road! What hopelessness permeated his last words:

"If I had the whole world, I would give it to live one day. I am about to take a leap in the dark!"

The good news is: Christians do not take leaps into the dark! When they die they go to Heaven!

Thomas Cromwell

Thomas Cromwell (1540), who became Earl of Essex, was the noted English statesman who was next to the King in power and influence. He was responsible for the digging up of the bones of Thomas Becket, and their burning as those of a traitor.

The Man Who Was Seduced

Over ambitious, Cromwell lost his influence and also his head, for he was executed. Historians tell us that as he died, he said in a speech:

"THE DEVIL IS READY TO SEDUCE US, AND I HAVE BEEN SEDUCED, but bear me witness that I die in the Catholic Faith."

Notice how people want to associate with God at the last moment. This man was insisting that he was in the faith!

Thomas Cork

Thomas Cork cried out in anguish as he was dying. He said, **"Until this moment I thought there was neither a God nor a devil. But now I know, and I feel that there are both."** He exclaimed, **"I am doomed to judgment by the judgment of the Almighty."**

Robert Green Ingersoll

He Wrote About the Mistakes of the Bible

Robert Green Ingersoll (1833-1899), famous American lawyer and prominent agnostic, lectured on *Biblical inaccuracies and contradictions.* His famed lecture "The Mistakes of Moses" led one defender of the Bible to say that he would like to hear Moses speak for five minutes on *The Mistakes of Ingersoll!*

Do I Have a Soul?

When he came to the gates of hell he was frozen with terror and he said, **"OH GOD, IF THERE IS A GOD, HAVE MERCY ON MY SOUL - IF I HAVE A SOUL."**

Sir Francis Gilfort

Sir Francis Gilfort, was taught early in his life about the gospel.

The Potential Minister Who Backslid

He was a backslidden Christian. In fact, it was expected that he would become a minister, **but he fell into bad company**. When he was passing on to eternity, he said,

"From where is this war in my heart? What arguments do I have to assist me in matters of fact? Do I say there is no hell when I feel one in my bosom?

AYE, AM I CERTAIN THAT THERE IS NO JUDGMENT WHEN I FEEL PRESENT JUDGMENT? Oh, wretch that I am. Whither shall I flee from this?

That there is a God, I know, for I continually feel that of His wrath. That there is a hell, I am surely certain.

Oh! That I was to lie upon the fire that never quench for a thousand years to purchase the favour of God, and to be reverted to Him again. But it is a fruitless wish.

Millions and millions of years will bring me no nearer to the end of my torment. Eternity, eternity!"

Do You Want Anyone to Pray For You?

As the distress of this man increased, he was asked whether he wanted some people to be invited to pray for him. He responded **"Tigers and monsters, are you devils to come to torment me? Will you give me the prospects of Heaven to make my hell more intolerable?"**

Then he said, **"Oh! the insufferable pangs of death."** And with that he died. How frightening!

William Pope

William Pope, was a born-again Christian, and knew the love of God. But he backslid when his wife died, and he followed Tom Paine. Not long after he backslid, he contracted tuberculosis, which was known at that time as The Consumption.

He is said to have been the leader of a company of infidels who ridiculed everything religious.

They Kicked the Bible and Tore it up

This was a classic backslider who said when he was dying, **"No case is comparable to mine, I cannot revert, God will damn me forever."**

One of the exercises of he and his friends was to kick the Bible about the floor, or tear it up. Friends who were present in his death-chamber spoke of it as a scene of terror.

A Frightening Scene of Death

His eyes rolled to and fro as he was dying on his bed, and he lifted up his hands as he cried out, **"I have no contrition. I cannot repent. God will damn me. I know the day of grace is past...You see one who is damned forever... Oh, Eternity! Eternity... Nothing for me but hell. Come, eternal torments... Do you not see? Do you not see him? He is coming for me. Oh! the burning flame, the hell, the pain that I feel. Eternity will explain my torment."**

And with these words, he died.

These were the very last words of a backslider!!

Dear Christian friend, what else can I say? I have shown you the real life testimonies of real people just like yourself. If that is not enough to make you believe and stay with God, then perhaps...

I have bargained for your soul, sharing with you all that a pastor can. I have shown you why you should not backslide. I have shown you the causes of backsliding, the descriptions of backsliding, and the symptoms of backsliding. I have shown you how people who backslide behave when they approach the gates of eternity. On the other hand, I have shown you the happy farewells of Christians with staying power to the very end.

My prayer for you is that you will find Christ and STAY in Christ. [77]For on Christ the solid rock we stand. Amen!!!